YANGA UNPLUGGED

PREMAL R. PATEL

YANGA UNPLUGGED

Your Actions Nourish Growth *Ambitions*

PREMAL R. PATEL

Yanga Unplugged
Copyright © 2025 Premal R. Patel
First published in 2025

Print: 978-1-76124-236-6
E-book: 978-1-76124-237-3
Hardback: 978-1-76124-238-0

All rights reserved. No part of this book may be reproduced, stored in a retrieval system, or transmitted by any means (electronic, mechanical, photocopying, recording, or otherwise) without written permission from the author.

Because of the dynamic nature of the Internet, any web addresses or links contained in this book may have changed since publication and may no longer be valid. The information in this book is based on the author's experiences and opinions. The views expressed in this book are solely those of the author and do not necessarily reflect the views of the publisher; the publisher hereby disclaims any responsibility for them.

The author of this book does not dispense any form of medical, legal, financial, or technical advice either directly or indirectly. The intent of the author is solely to provide information of a general nature to help you in your quest for personal development and growth. In the event you use any of the information in this book, the author and the publisher assume no responsibility for your actions. If any form of expert assistance is required, the services of a competent professional should be sought.

Publishing information
Publishing and design facilitated by Passionpreneur Publishing
A division of Passionpreneur Organization Pty Ltd
ABN: 48640637529

Melbourne, VIC | Australia
www.passionpreneurpublishing.com

To my Fathers, forever my inspiration and guiding light

TABLE OF CONTENTS

Acknowledgements

Testimonials

Chapter 1
THE VOICE OF GUIDANCE: A SON'S JOURNEY
THROUGH TRIUMPHS AND TRIALS

Chapter 2
LET'S GET TO THE YANGA: IT'S ALL ABOUT SELF-BELIEF –
YOU ARE IN CONTROL

Chapter 3
THE POWER OF TAKING ACTION: SURROUND YOURSELF
WITH THE RIGHT ENERGY-BOOSTERS

Chapter 4
EMBRACE HARD TIMES: ADVERSITY REWIRES
OUR BRAIN

Chapter 5
SEEDS OF GROWTH: CHILDHOOD EXPERIENCES
SHAPE OUR MINDSET

Chapter 6
PATH TO AMBITION: THINKING TOO FAR AHEAD DOESN'T WORK

Chapter 7
NOT EVERY SETBACK IS THE END OF THE STORY: PEOPLE RISE FROM PERSONAL FAILURES

Chapter 8
THE POWER OF SELF-BELIEF: BELIEVING IN YOURSELF IS THE FIRST STEP TO FULFILLING YOUR AMBITIONS

Chapter 9
THE PARALYSING GRIP OF OVERTHINKING: MIND TRAPS MUST BE REFRAMED AND SIMPLIFIED

Chapter 10
FROM WORRIER TO ACCEPTOR: EMBRACING LIFE'S UNCERTAINTIES AND CONSERVING ENERGY

Chapter 11
NAVIGATING CONVERSATIONS FROM INNER THOUGHTS TO OUTER VOICES: CONVERSATIONS THAT SHAPE US

Chapter 12
THE DOUBLE-EDGED SWORD OF AI: HOPE, EXCITEMENT AND FEAR

Conclusion

Works Cited

Author Bio

Resources and Important Links

ACKNOWLEDGEMENTS

I am deeply indebted to my Fathers (RG and GR) for teaching me valuable lessons early on in my life. I am grateful for the teachers who encouraged me not to think beyond what they taught, as they influenced me to break the rules. My deepest appreciation for my family and those I love for supporting my journey and putting up with me over the years (it has not been easy for them). Finally, a special thank you to the team at Passionpreneur Publishing for believing in my story and championing it tirelessly.

TESTIMONIALS

'Prem Patel is an exceptional people's person and networker. I had the good fortune to have benefited from his business development skills two decades ago when he managed growth for BPG out of Dubai. I would call Prem a glass always half full—brimming with positive energy and optimism that is hugely infectious. Over the years, while he has matured, his positive energy and 'never say never' spirit has not waned. I would personally rate him as one of the most positive people I have come across in my four-decades-plus professional career.'
—AVI BHOJANI, GROUP CEO BPG GROUP

'Heartfelt and authentic—many people can learn from Premal's words of wisdom intertwined with the legacy from his own father-figures.'
—NICOLE SOAMES, AUTHOR AND CEO DIADEM

'Don't hesitate—jump right into this very readable, actionable and honest guide book for life! In the many years I've known and worked with Prem, he has been a positive, thoughtful, and engaging individual who makes stuff happen, someone that you want to spend time with and have on your team. Now I know why—it's his YANGA!'

—JEREMY NICHOLDS, EXECUTIVE LEADER

'Premal Patel combines his poignant personal stories and life experiences with leadership lessons distilled from a career spanning three continents to deliver a highly readable and compelling guide on how to take purposeful action to achieve one's career and life ambitions.'

—RAVI CHATURVEDI, MANAGING DIRECTOR, DIGITAL PLANET, THE FLETCHER SCHOOL OF LAW AND DIPLOMACY, TUFTS UNIVERSITY

'YANGA Unplugged is more than a book—it's a reflection of who Prem is as a leader and a human. Authentic, grounded, and deeply intentional. His personal journey gives powerful context to the way he lifts others. This book is a spark—it challenges you to dig deep, believe in yourself, and take meaningful action toward the growth and life you desire.'

—TRICIA MANNING, EXECUTIVE COACH, AUTHOR OF *LEAD WITH HEART* AND *LEAVE A LEGACY*

'Prem's stories and insights were very meaningful to me, especially his message that putting yourself first is not selfish, but essential. In a world where we are taught to think of others, sometimes at the cost of our own aspirations, his words are both liberating and necessary. What I found most meaningful was how Prem's experiences, from overcoming adversity to building self-belief, are universal. His journey mirrors the resilience and adaptability that so many of us in small communities must embrace. This book is a heartfelt call to action: to trust ourselves, to keep learning, and to never let fear or age limit our ambitions. YANGA Unplugged is more than a guide; it's a celebration of the enduring human spirit. It reminds us that even as our communities change, our capacity for hope and reinvention remains undiminished.'

—MAZARINE MEMON, ARTIST AND ENTREPRENEUR

'After reading Prem's book, the tune won't leave my head: 'Let's Go Do The YANGA'! Indeed, let's do it. By using personal storytelling, wrapped in the energy of a radical memoir, Prem uses the value in vulnerability to challenge traditional structures in business & life. Throughout his book, he selflessly encourages the reader to look inside to understand the true meaning of the collective stretch. A stretch that starts with self, of course, especially when it comes to that 'common commonality' … perfectionism. I love that Prem challenges perfection and its naughty friend procrastination in favour of 'doing right in the moment'. I also appreciate the energy of his writing using powerful, useful, helpful lived experiences, as well as sharing simple, smart action steps. From passive dreams to active actions. Let's Unplug YANGA.'

—SUSAN FURNESS, ALTERNATIVE STRATEGIST, AUTHOR AND COACH

CHAPTER 1
THE VOICE OF GUIDANCE: A SON'S JOURNEY THROUGH TRIUMPHS AND TRIALS

'I nurture harmony and peace in the world, while honouring my own voice and inner strength.'

YANGA is a term commonly used in some African cultures to describe a strong sense of self-confidence, pride, and assertiveness. It represents a bold and assertive attitude towards life, often characterised by a display of resilience, courage and determination. In the Zulu culture, it holds significance and evokes a sense of strength, power and resilience.

Before I get into the core of YANGA Unplugged, I'm taking you back to 30th March 1970 to share a personal story with you. Being emotional and open does not come easily to me, so bear with me. Over the last few years, however, I have begun to understand the importance of being more open and honest about how I feel, my beliefs, and what I want in life.

My father—RG—a popular, smart, and ambitious character with poise and presence, was a man who always put others first. Whilst a banker by profession working for Standard Bank in Nairobi, Kenya (East Africa), his true passion was cricket. He loved the game, playing for Nairobi's Premier Cricket Club and helping them win many tournaments and trophies. Always a player to watch, he leaves the impressive legacy of scoring the fastest century, which he accomplished in just 40 minutes. At 24, he had his whole life ahead of him when he married his beautiful wife, aged 16. (Yes, that's correct, 16, as you could do that back in India in those days.) Very soon, they had my sister in 1966; I came along in 1969. (Now you all know how old I am.)

The highly ambitious RG wanted to provide a better life for his children, as Kenya was a tough place to make it big in the corporate banking world (especially for people of Asian descent). In early 1970, RG received a confirmation to transfer to England with Standard Bank in June of that year. This was big news, as England (specifically London) was a dreamland for many East-African Asians who wanted to work hard and build a better life for their families.

As you can imagine, everyone in our family was celebrating. Crucially, two important actions would now take place. Firstly, my father would move his family to London, UK and start a new life with a promising corporate career. Secondly, my grandfather—GR (he was actually known as GR Barclays Bank, having completed 30 years of service) would fulfil his ambition to move back to India for his retirement with my grandmother. (Both had been away from India and their families since the early 1940s.)

Knowing his cricketing days would now be over, my father resolved to play as much as he could before boarding the aircraft and saying goodbye to all his friends and siblings in Nairobi. The Premier Club Management would miss his presence and flair for the game, especially as the Kenyan Cricket Team scouts were watching him closely, but understood his reason to go—family first.

On 29th March 1970, RG was playing his last tournament, in Mombasa, for Premier Cricket Club. As this was a major cup game, it was an important one to win (both for RG himself to leave on a high, and for the club in terms of the league). They won, and RG captained their win as expected. It was celebrations all round. As the winning captain, he could leave with his head held high and trophy in hand.

CELEBRATING THE HUMAN CONNECTIONS THAT UNITE US

On 29th March 1970, RG was in the passenger seat of a vehicle as he and another player from the winning team drove back from Mombasa to Nairobi. RG was holding the winning trophy as they talked about the game. It was nightfall, and the roads from Mombasa to Nairobi were very dark with no streetlights. The roads were rough, so I doubt they had a smooth ride. Back then, large trucks would quite often park up on the side of highways so drivers could rest after long journeys. Some would remain in their vehicles, while others would sleep under a cover placed over their trucks, which were usually dark in colour.

Then, in a split second—BANG—it was all over.

RG's vehicle hit a covered truck at full speed. Although the driver tried swerving to avoid impact, it was unavoidable. With the impact occurring on the passenger side, my father was seriously injured at only 31 years of age. After the impact, there was only silence. They were in the middle of nowhere, with both men's families waiting for them to return home and celebrate the win.

Now, imagine the scene at home. As they waited to celebrate, my father's family found out about the accident through a close family friend—but not the extent of his injuries. My grandfather, grandmother and uncle quickly travelled to the hospital in Mombasa where paramedics had taken my father. When they arrived, my father was in critical condition. At this stage my mother was unaware of what had happened. The next day, my mother arrived in a state of panic, spending time with my father by his bedside before returning home to her children. When she reached them, she received the news that my father had passed away. It was 30th March, 1970.

Everyone was shocked. My stunned mother was completely still, widowed at just 22, with a two-and-a-half year old daughter and me at just 10 months. Obviously, at that age I had no idea what was going on; I simply demanded my mother's time and attention whilst she was traumatised, not knowing what to do. What must have been going through my mother's mind? Only she knows. As for my grandparents, losing their eldest son in such a way would make even the most resilient and strong-minded person fall apart.

It was the human connections, the community around my family, that got them through the dark days that followed. My father's death brought his parents closer to my mother—they lived by the mantra, 'We're in it together.'

ADAPTING TO CHANGE AND NAVIGATING NEW REALITIES

What happened next was nothing short of amazing. My grandfather, GR, a man with a strong presence and a deeply caring personality, decided to follow through with my father's ambition to move to the UK. He negotiated a move to London with Barclays Bank, where he could continue working until he was 65 (UK retirement age at that time). Imagine his resilient mindset—having been all ready to pack up and move back to India after what must have felt as a lifetime in Nairobi, Kenya, he had to manage a major turnaround in his and his family's life overnight.

After we moved to the UK in June 1971, GR started working for Barclays in London while my mother (who was fragile, but strong-willed and determined) started working in retail. Imagine her situation. Having not worked a day in her life up to that point, as my father had taken care of her, here she was taking her first job in London, when English was not her first language. For that reason, she is also a true inspiration to me.

I have thought about my father every day for the last 55 years, and probably will until my last day in this beautiful world. Thinking of him makes my world a better place. Yet I never talked to him, never heard his voice, do not remember a single facial expression, and never hugged him or held his hand. However, I *hear* him—a voice inside my head guiding me, advising me, even scolding me when I have misbehaved.

My grandfather became my father figure, and there has been no one else like him. His courage, kindness, and big personality live inside me every day. After my father's death, he understandably wanted the simple things in life (peace, love, and laughter). He lived to protect his remaining family by providing them with a secure, loving environment, with his biggest ambition being to enable a solid educational foundation for my sister and me. His dream, then, was to fulfil my father's dream.

SO, LET'S GO BACK TO THE BEGINNING AND TALK ABOUT YANGA UNPLUGGED.

I was aggressively driven in my early years, an attitude which I feel comes down to the tough environment where I grew up. For example, from age eleven I woke up every Sunday morning at 7 am to work in a market with my uncle and cousin selling doormats and flooring. I earned £3 for each shift, saving some cash to help with household bills in the process. My desire to support my family was deeply embedded in my DNA.

In my late teens and early 20s, I was driven, yet calm and understanding. The vague knowledge I had of my father, coupled with the persistent desire to know more about him and his life, shaped me as a person—as the father at home, the leader at work, the coach and facilitator I aspired to be, and the successful entrepreneur I wanted to become. All these roles were carefully blended in a way that placed others first, putting their needs before mine (especially my family's). By living these values, I hoped to make my father feel proud of me.

My story highlights resilience, courage and determination, while signifying strength and power.

FROM DOUBT TO DETERMINATION

From the very beginning, the world felt different for me. Losing my father at just ten months old meant that the man who should have been a guiding light in my life was but a distant memory, a figure viewed through the lens of family stories and faded photographs. Yet in the quiet moments when life's challenges loomed large, I often found myself leaning into an inner dialogue, one infused with the wisdom and love of the father I never knew.

As I embarked on my turbulent journey into the business world, during which I faced many obstacles, I often thought about what my father would say. My first graduate job was with a bank, where I received three promotions in a short time. When I went for a more senior role four years into my career (having already moved from branch banking to Marketing in Head Office), I was passed over for the promotion for being too young. Feeling the sting of not being able to achieve the growth I craved, doubt began to creep in. While wrestling with feelings of inadequacy, I recalled the voice that had become my anchor. 'Learn from this, Premal. Every setback is an opportunity to grow. This is just the beginning.' Slowly but surely, I built a powerful network and reputation, emerging stronger than before.

Through the ups and downs, I often found myself reflecting on the lessons I believed my father would have taught me, and on the lessons imparted by my grandfather. For example,

I feel my father would have said, 'Have courage and be kind to others.'

I realise I have many stories to share—my failures, my triumphs, and the lessons learned along the way. When I speak about resilience and strength of mind, I recall and echo the words that have guided me and which I have internalised over the years—a harmonious blend of my own experiences and the wisdom I attribute to my father.

OUR STRENGTH DETERMINES OUR JOURNEY

There are moments when I realise that while I never knew my father in life, the voice within me has become a powerful guide, shaping my choices, providing comfort during dark times, and inspiring me to strive for greatness—yes, there is more to come from me, as my journey is not over. The journey has not been easy, but it *has* been meaningful, a testament to the strength of family bonds that transcend time and loss.

As I started thinking through my story and connecting it to today's volatile, uncertain, and often unsettling world, I realised that YANGA Unplugged can help others who are going through personal or career crises make the transition a little easier to cope with. For years, I felt I was invincible and didn't need anyone's help to achieve success. Unfortunately, that didn't get me very far.

We cannot win alone. Conversation—*real* conversation—is more urgent now, and human connectivity is the central factor which will help us thrive as a community, both today and well into the future.

My life so far has been a journey of learning to balance my desire for harmony with my need for personal strength and self-expression. My deeper spiritual challenge is learning to stand firm in my truth.

The rest of this book is focused on YANGA, specifically how we can unplug my own experience in life and business to help you take action and achieve professional success, emotional fulfilment and spiritual growth. In this sense, it is important to know that YANGA can stand for **Your Actions Nourish Growth Ambitions**.

As I conclude, I understand that my North Star is not merely a destination but a continuous journey of growth, learning, and connection to my roots—whether I will ever reach it, only God knows. Through the challenges and victories, I have forged a path that honours my father's and grandfather's legacy while carving out my own identity.

For many years, I put others' needs before my own, which probably came from my grandfather telling me that I should always 'think of others'. As this was also my primary school's motto, the same message consumed me for many years.

YANGA (YOUR ACTIONS NOURISH GROWTH AMBITIONS)

Put yourself at the forefront of your focus. Take action, experiment, and try new things. Provide your brain with energy-boosters while reducing or eliminating the energy-drainers. Grow your world and yourself while sharing your stories and fulfilling your dreams. Life is short, and can be taken from us in an instant.

The first 'tough love' messages:

1. If you are waiting for someone to save you, you will wait forever. No one is coming.
2. You make your own choices, so be prepared to accept the outcomes.
3. You have the courage—so find it, then live your best life every day.

CHAPTER 2

LET'S GET TO THE YANGA: IT'S ALL ABOUT SELF-BELIEF – YOU ARE IN CONTROL

There are two things that make a dream impossible to achieve:

1. The fear of failure, and
2. Thinking of everyone else.

At my primary school, all I could see was a large board saying 'Think of Others.' At home, we were often taught to think of everybody else. What will everyone else think? What will they say? You must behave. Don't embarrass us. But really, you can't think about others until you start thinking about yourself. By putting yourself first, you are in a better position to achieve your ambitions while supporting others to achieve their dreams.

Without *personal* clarity, you will not have clarity on how to best support others. Consequently, your initial goal should be to figure yourself out. This chapter is all about you and your actions, and being in the right frame of mind to deal with the challenges in your world that prevent you from achieving your ambitions.

You have probably been told, or read in books, that you can absolutely achieve anything you want. They're not wrong. We can all climb Mount Kilimanjaro, but it takes hard work, time, and focused training with experts to make it happen. I'm hearing you now saying, 'I have a day job, a family, a community—they need me around.' That's your choice. If you have bigger dreams and ambitions, though, you may need to step back and consider alternatives.

FOR A FULFILLING LIFE, EMBRACE YOUR DREAMS

Dreams and ambitions are vital to our existence, driving enhanced performance, focus, motivation, and joy in achievement. Though we can't always fully realise our dreams, the mere act of pursuing them moves us forward.

How we choose to spend our 24 daily hours makes all the difference. Time spent in idle activities like excessive TV watching could be better utilised. The common excuse of having 'not enough time' is simply that—an *excuse*, masking a lack of action.

I know this firsthand. I've used that very excuse repeatedly on my own book project, which has now stretched on for nearly three years. Job demands, family commitments, and a desire for rest have all contributed to the delays. But the reality is, I could have made more meaningful progress if I had overcome those excuses.

PUTTING 'YOU' FIRST IS NOT SELFISH

If I consider today's world, the corporate world is very demanding. You have to put customers, employees, and your boss first, make your board happy, and make your peers happy. Yet no one ever really talks about putting yourself first. It's often seen as selfish, but it's actually not. When you reflect on your own needs, you are then in a much better place to attend to those of others, so putting yourself first is probably the most unselfish thing you can do. It helps you take ownership of your own life as a priority and focus on the important things that matter to you. We are constantly steered by everyone else's opinions, ending up with self-imposed barriers and finding excuses to avoid spending time with ourselves and our needs. For years, you can become cluttered with other people's thoughts, opinions, observations, and comments.

AI, advancing technology, and smarter ways of working make everything feel faster…and you need to keep up. Many people suffer from FOBO—the 'fear of becoming obsolete', which is actually happening in today's world. (FOMO is yesterday's news.) If you don't spend time on yourself, you cannot reinvent yourself, upskill, transform how you learn, or improve the way you complete your everyday tasks. Time is precious and always running out.

TO ACHIEVE YOUR GOALS, MASTER SELF-BELIEF AND SELF-CONTROL

There are two important skills which will enable you to achieve whatever you want. I doubt any one of us would achieve our ambitions without these, as many influences, blockers, and barriers would get in the way—especially those in your mind. The two important skills are:

1. Self-belief, and
2. Self-control.

FROM DOUBT TO DETERMINATION

Back in the early '70s, I attended a primary school in London. It was a lovely establishment with a good reputation, which came highly recommended. I hated it. I was the only Asian student (or at least it felt like that at the time), coming from a single-parent family, whereas all the other students had the perfect family environment. I was teased often by other kids who made fun of me for not having a father, for wearing glasses, for being Asian. They called me names which cut through me like a sharp knife.

I would often hide just to get away and avoid listening to the abuse. Tears would quite often be rolling down my eyes as I simply couldn't talk to anyone about the situation—I didn't know how to. At home, I was always told to remain quiet. The teachers wouldn't listen to me, often claiming that I was making up stories. I didn't really want to share my problems with my mother and my family who were trying to cope in a new community, and probably felt out of place themselves. My self-belief as a young Asian boy in a very white area was at rock bottom.

To be honest, at that time I didn't even know what self-belief was. I lacked confidence and became very closed off and quiet. (For those who know me now, this will no doubt come as a big surprise.) Every day, I would wait for the final bell to ring so I could run to my grandmother, who'd always make me feel better with a little treat as I walked home. When you are that young, it's very difficult to openly share what is happening. I often thought that this was simply what happens everywhere in the world, and I just needed to get used to it.

My self-belief then took a further battering when I moved to high school.

With racism rife at this time, every day I would run home trying to avoid the bullies on the way. 'Trying' was the operative word here, and I wasn't very successful, considering I had a 30-minute walk (which was probably a 15-minute run) to get home.

The bullies were everywhere, and the racial abuse, coupled with the taunts about my father not being around, hit me like a barrage of missiles. I would often get home with my school tie cut and trousers ripped, along with glue and other liquids like Tip-Ex (white correction fluid) sprayed all over my blazer. It felt like I was in hell…and I had four more years to go.

One day when I really couldn't take anymore, I summoned the courage to openly discuss what was going on with my grandfather, GR. He listened, gave me a hug, and said, 'Everything will be all right.' In that moment, I felt different, protected; confidence started to run through my veins.

GR was a simple man of few words. I recall a time when we used to live on top of a shop and he ran after some vandals who had thrown a brick through the shop window and into our apartment. He caught one of them and held onto him until the police turned up. (I was watching him.) From that day on, our windows were never broken and the thugs stayed away. In his concluding remarks, he told me that I need to take control of the situation, or the situation would control me. He inspired me to overcome my fears, explaining that most of the time, bullies attack others because they're envious and weak of mind.

I walked away from that conversation a little scared of the unknown, uncertain whether I had the strength to make a change. When I stuck up to the bullies (or tried to), things got worse for a short while—but they were dealing with a new me. That conversation with GR, and some of the conversations I had with my inner voice (RG), helped me turn a corner in my self-belief, pushing me to overcome my adversity soon after. My self-belief helped me take control of the situation and achieve the desired outcome. The bullying lessened, then stopped over the years, which was a valuable lesson for me whilst at high school. I had taken control of the situation and successfully changed the outcome.

This self-belief soon transitioned into my academic career. Never the brightest student, I always had to work very hard to achieve average grades. By the time I reached university, though, my confidence and self-belief soared. Believing I could achieve more and take control of my time empowered me to improve my results and achieve a university diploma, followed by a degree. This was the dream of my Fathers, whose self-belief provided the foundation to overcome life's challenges.

Self-belief, then, is more than just confidence. It runs much deeper, providing an unshakable conviction that you are capable of navigating life's difficulties and achieving your goals no matter what stands in your way.

BELIEVE IN YOUR OWN POTENTIAL

In March 1970, things got very tough for my family. I often think about the self-belief my grandfather, GR, needed to have in order to confidently handle such a difficult situation. With the whole family leaning on him for emotional support, he must have had broad shoulders; having just lost his eldest son, he now had to navigate a new world as he planned to move to the UK with his son's very young family, placing them in a foreign country and educating the children in an alien environment. By doing so, he showed that he had the inner resources to figure things out, learn, and grow.

Two things my grandfather shared with me have stuck in my mind since I was a child. These are:

1. **Trust yourself.** Believe you can succeed and adapt to any challenges that arise.
2. **Believe in your potential.** You may not have all the answers today, but you have the capacity to learn and improve.

In my early twenties, I faced still more turbulent times. In 1994, my grandfather passed away suddenly as a result of a brain aneurysm. There was so much we still needed to talk about, so much I wanted to show him and prove to him. We had no time to say goodbye.

When he died at 1:00 am on 27th August 1994, there were no parting words between us, just like my father and grandfather back in March 1970. He died in my arms within minutes. My world, and my family's world, crumbled again. Now, though, I didn't have a father figure to provide direction, guidance, and advice, or to share my thoughts, my pain, or my ideas with. I had to be strong and brave for the rest of my family.

Self-belief kept me grounded, enabled me to move forward. What it *really* does is prevent you from being swept away by doubt, fear or uncertainty—self-belief breeds resilience. With resilience, you start to see setbacks and failures as temporary (a moment in time), simply part of life's journey. We need to embrace them and find the strength to keep going. (Remember YANGA, Your Actions Nourish Growth Ambitions.)

YOU ARE IN CONTROL OF YOUR ACTIONS

In life, one of the most empowering realisations is that you are in control. It doesn't always feel that way, I know. There are people who can influence outcomes, and unexpected challenges can blindside you. Yet at the core of it all, you are in control of how you respond, the decisions you make, and the direction you take. Understanding this at a deep level is the key to living a fulfilled and purpose-driven life. Three important factors enable you to gain more control:

1. Your mindset,
2. Your actions, and
3. Your reactions.

Control over your mindset: You cannot always control the events happening around you (my father's accident was out of his control), but you can always control your mindset. It's how you perceive and interpret the world. You may not always understand why certain events happened to you, but your thoughts shape your emotions and drive your actions—which create your reality.

Control over your actions: This means taking responsibility for what you can do and how. Only you control your actions, the steps you take towards your goal, the effort you put in each day, and the decisions you make in the face of adversity. Focusing on what you can control—your actions—gives you the freedom to achieve good outcomes.

Control over your reactions: Life is unfortunately unpredictable, and challenges are inevitable, but what makes the difference between thriving and merely surviving is how you react to things you can't control. You have control over your reactions (it's like a superpower). By controlling reactions, you protect your inner peace and maintain focus on what truly matters, even in chaotic times.

SELF-EMPOWERMENT IS THE FOUNDATION TO BEING IN CONTROL

When you realise you hold the reins to your thoughts, actions and responses, you no longer see yourself as the victim of life's circumstances. Instead, you become an active participant in your own journey, fully accountable for the results you create. This sense of self-empowerment builds three important capabilities, each of which help you own your life story.

These are:

1. **Self-confidence.** Knowing that you are in control builds confidence.
2. **Freedom.** As control brings freedom, you no longer seek external validation.
3. **Resilience.** When you control how you respond to adversity, you become more resilient.

Over the years, I have realised that my life is my responsibility. External factors may influence my journey, but I'm the driver of my actions and my future. At the heart of self-belief is having a strong forward-thinking mindset, without limitations.

Two important factors will enhance this mindset.

1. **Effort leads to success.** People with a growth mindset believe that success comes from effort, not luck. This enables you to embrace challenges and opportunities to grow. You view obstacles as part of the process and not a dead end.
2. **Learn from failure.** Don't see failure as a reflection of your capabilities—see it as a learning experience instead. Failure is not the end, but a stepping stone to improvement.

Without self-belief, even the most talented, knowledgeable, or well-prepared individual can falter in the face of adversity. Self-belief is what keeps you moving forward when others give up.

TO LIVE A TRULY EMPOWERED LIFE:

1. You must own your choices, mistakes, growth, and success. When you do this, it is truly liberating.
2. Know you have the power to shape your life, no matter your past or present circumstances. When you embrace this power, you step into the driver's seat of your life.
3. Create a future that reflects your values, aspirations, and authentic self. Life is not about what happens to you—it's about how much self-belief and control (ownership) you have and how you choose to show up in the face of it all.

So at this point, stop, take a step back, and do a mind audit:

- What would it take for you to better control your mindset, actions, and reactions?
- How important is achieving your dreams and ambitions?
- Are you ready to make some hard choices if need be?

CHANGING DIRECTION AND TAKING MORE CONTROL MEANS YOU'LL HAVE TO DEAL WITH SOME HARD CHOICES

As we navigate through this book, remember what YANGA Unplugged stands for—Your Actions Nourish Growth Ambitions. In every chapter, I will share a lesson learned, which can serve as a framework you can apply to your life. That's because everything starts with you. You can't expect anyone else to do things for you. It's all about you, and remember—you are in control.

Here, let me offer a brief overview of what's contained in subsequent chapters:

Chapter 3: The Power of Taking Action
Examine your internal and external energy influences, identifying energy-drainers and energy-boosters to create a more positive environment.

Chapter 4: Embrace Hard Times
Tough times are growth opportunities. Nourish your brain to make better choices and decisions.

Chapter 5: Seeds of Growth
Learn to handle the impact of others' opinions, while taking responsibility for your personal development.

Chapter 6: Path to Ambition
Discover your true ambitions, but don't overthink the path. Self-compassion is key.

Chapter 7: Not Every Setback is the End of the Story
View setbacks as chances to accelerate growth. Learn from mistakes and those who've supported you.

Chapter 8: The Power of Self-Belief
Understand how self-belief drives resilience and courage—the foundations of growth.

Chapter 9: The Paralysing Grip of Overthinking
Reframe your thinking to simplify decision-making and avoid overthinking.

Chapter 10: From Worrier to Acceptor
Embrace the reality that some changes will go wrong. Enjoy the journey and see each experience as a life lesson.

Chapter 11: Navigating Conversations from Inner Thoughts to Outer Voices
Develop the crucial skill of intentional, authentic communication to create real connections.

Chapter 12: The Double-Edged Sword of AI
AI is a double-edged sword—so use it to reinvent your life and improve human connections.

Each chapter will end with a few 'tough love' messages, starting here:

- The only person who doubts your self-belief is you.
- The only person who creates limiting beliefs is you.

- The only person who can take action to reduce limiting beliefs is you.

Again, it's all about you, so taking action is the only way you can move forward. Stop dwelling on the past, think ahead, and consider the beautiful world you can create starting today. What does your future look like now? Can you visualise it?

Then, take action as your first step. **YANGA—Your Actions Nourish Growth Ambitions**.

CHAPTER 3

THE POWER OF TAKING ACTION: SURROUND YOURSELF WITH THE RIGHT ENERGY-BOOSTERS

'THERE IS NO PERFECTION, ONLY A SERIES OF MOMENTS THAT COME TOGETHER TO CREATE A BEAUTIFUL STORY.'

—PAULO COELHO, *THE ALCHEMIST*

There is only one way to learn—through action. In our fast-paced and volatile world, taking action is a critical skill to master. It is your actions, and how you execute them, that create an impact. We all have ideas, aspirations, and good intentions, yet what truly matters is how we transform these thoughts into tangible outcomes and demonstrate progress. No one remembers all the talk—they remember what we have done.

NAVIGATING AN UNCERTAIN AND OFTEN NEGATIVE WORLD

Our world is in flux. Markets shift rapidly and we experience content overload, creating paralysis. So, remain relevant and keep growing by taking action and getting stuff done. We are all surrounded by so many negative influences and opinions, whether from our family, our friends, people at work, or people we have just met. Everybody has a perspective, and everyone has opinions about what we should do and how we should do it.

One of the hardest things to do is to cut the negatives from your life. The important things are to navigate your journey and surround yourself with positive energy-boosters.

THE ESSENTIAL ROLE OF ENERGY-BOOSTERS IN ENHANCING WELLBEING AND PRODUCTIVITY

These are people who motivate you, who inspire you, or things that make you feel good, that create a positive impact in your mind so you can get things done in a very positive and confident manner. Most important in your life is how you energise yourself. It's all about you. Only you can decide whether you surround yourself with those energy-drainers or energy-boosters. Energy boosters inspire us, providing us with confidence so we can take leaps forward towards achieving our ambitions and our dreams. Remember, everything around you impacts and influences your energy.

Your most precious commodities are your time and energy. You choose where to use your time and how to invest your energy, yet you often waste this power. Precious hours are lost in over-analysing, overthinking, and comparing yourself with what you see on social media. That's your choice.

SEIZE THE MOMENT. IF YOU WAIT, YOU WILL BE HELD BACK FROM LIVING

Finding the perfect time to do something, or over-analysing, can lead to missed opportunities. Actions create momentum, which builds success. Many of you may feel the need to be a perfectionist, but the truth is this is a total waste of time—it is time to alter your thinking if you are on that path. Perfection is actually unachievable as there's always a better way; improvements can always be made. So it is all about speed, which trumps perfection; we must learn to act even when conditions are not ideal.

ACT NOW, DON'T WAIT

The ability to act quickly and then adjust is more valuable than committing to a rigid course of action. Taking action allows you to feel, learn, and adapt in real time.

Let's do an exercise now, where we consider what drains your energy. **List five to six energy-drainers which you have or are experiencing. Then, consider what makes them so draining and what you need to do to change them.** (You may not have the exact answer for the last column, but it's worth having a go at this stage.)

Energy-drainers in my life	What makes them so draining?	What do I need to change now?

Then, list what energises you and creates that spark in your day, week, month—and why.

What energises me?	Why do I feel energised?	How can I get more of these energy-boosters or find new ones?

ARE YOU SURROUNDED BY MORE ENERGY-BOOSTERS OR ENERGY-DRAINERS?

Energy is a currency in our fast-paced lives that demand so much of us, so ask yourself a question: How much time have you spent on investing in positive energy this month? It's a bit like getting your salary each month, then budgeting for certain household expenditures like food, rent, bills, and entertainment. How much of the energy you have each month are you investing in your self-learning, your self-development, your motivation, things that inspire you, and things that help you achieve your ambitions and goals?

You must stay mentally neutral and straightforwardly take action in order to move from energy-drainers to energy-boosters—but remember that the clock is ticking. You can never regain lost time, and if you don't take positive action now, nothing will change.

INACTION DOESN'T SHAPE YOUR PATH TO SUCCESS

I worked for a company which had immense pride about their capacity for innovation, yet failed to execute this capacity. Due to the simple fact that the leaders wanted everything to be perfect before each project went live, they lost thousands in potential revenue.

While working there, I led a project aiming to fast-track the way we delivered marketing campaigns. With our customers demanding faster service at lower cost, we needed to inject more agility and flexibility into our delivery processes.

We started the project, yet over-analysed everything. We attended hours of calls and meetings, often discussing the same issue over and over again with the senior stakeholder team. Although our senior stakeholders wanted to innovate and improve, they were unwilling to commit to action until they saw the perfect plan (complete with Excel sheets containing detailed forecasts). Meanwhile, my team was ready to take immediate action and try something new, with 80% confidence that it would work. We decided to stop the project over a year later, as our customers had purchased a similar solution from a competitor to the one we had already designed. We knew we had the right solution, but other people's precautions caused us to become stuck in planning mode.

Returning now to my personal story, my grandfather, GR, took swift action when he heard the tragic news about my father's accident in March 1970. He quickly navigated the family through the rapid change required, altered his plans, and within a few weeks had a clear idea on how he was going to leave Nairobi and start a new life in London with the family. We had nowhere to move into, nor did we know our way around in the UK—but GR had a workable plan, which was worth the gamble.

In the process, he overcame any fear and avoided standing still. What I've realised over the years is that many of those I come across hesitate to act because they fear making a decision that doesn't come off, which would incur others' judgment. Yet in a world that changes so quickly, the real risk is not failing—it's standing still. The idea that you can wait until you are fully prepared, or 100% certain about success, reflects an outdated mindset.

Two important shifts in thinking will help you rethink how you perceive failure and overcome any fear of it. These are:

1. **We live in a world where we need to learn faster.** The faster you take action and experience the consequences, the quicker you can learn what works and what doesn't.
2. **Reframe your thinking from failure to growth.** Failure offers insights and lessons that you don't get from

success. It is through trying, failing and recalibrating that you're able to develop resilience, adaptability, and problem-solving skills.

TAKING ACTION HAS AN INCREDIBLE WAY OF CREATING CLARITY

Too often, people hesitate because they don't have all the answers or fear uncertainty, but consider this: You can't think your way to clarity. Instead, you have to *act* your way to it—action helps you discover what works, what excites you, and what doesn't. It helps you understand *yourself*. I've worked for many leading global organisations, and knew my time was up when I was expected to have all the answers before we even tried something new.

As you take action, your path becomes clearer. (It did for me.) Every step revealed new information and insights, opened new doors and relationships, and helped me navigate my next move. I took control of my career journey by taking bold actions, which I then repeated to build more self-confidence. Every time you take a step forward, regardless of the outcome, you build a sense of accomplishment while bolstering your sense of confidence in your ability to navigate challenges.

BREAK FREE FROM OVERTHINKING

Our world features an abundance of options, data, and opinions, which means we can all fall into the 'analysis paralysis' trap, leading to missed opportunities. When starting my career, I worked for a reputable global financial services brand where the culture involved over-analysing everything. At one point, I became an advocate of overthinking and started sharing the business mantra with new team members. One day when we were working under extreme pressure, I was looking for inspiration and motivation—surely, I thought, there was a better way of doing our work.

So, I decided to take the initiative and share a presentation on how we could reduce analysis paralysis and get things done faster, thus improving productivity and driving workplace efficiency. Well, my career was short-lived—not because I was fired, but because I felt compelled to resign. The company's leadership disagreed with my actions, as they felt I was creating too much disruption to their set ways. (These had been successful so far, so why change the status quo?) It was one of my best decisions.

I was now free from a culture that I was unsuited to, one that didn't want others to feel empowered. Moving on enabled me to try a new company, which embraced change, disruption, and new thinking. The one thing I'm *not* is an overthinker (well, not anymore). What I realised over time is that imperfect action beats perfect inaction every time. You don't need all the information to make progress. By taking small steps forward, you gain experience and knowledge that no amount of analysis can provide.

By contrast, standing still causes you to fall behind, lose relevance, and potentially miss out on growth. Every moment of inaction carries a cost of unseized opportunities.

EXPERIMENTATION, THE KEY TO GROWTH AND SUCCESS

Having the ability to experiment and pivot is crucial in today's world; some of you are probably even pivoting without realising it. We are talking about action, which is not just about working harder, but also about working smarter and trying new things. I live by two rules when it comes to action and experimentation, which I have learned the hard way along my journey. These are:

1. **Start before you are ready.** Sometimes the best way to figure out if something works or not is simply by trying it. You can improve and refine as you go. Waiting to be ready with all the resources in place is a recipe for standing still.
2. **Take small incremental wins.** Not every action needs to be massive. Sometimes, the greatest joy and progress comes from small experiments. A single action today compounds into bigger wins tomorrow.

Time and energy are both precious commodities under your control. Whatever you do, enjoy your time and invest your energy thoughtfully. If you are fixated on the goal (which is easy to do in today's results-obsessed world), you may lose sight of the lessons, growth and experiences gained on the journey. Conversely, by embracing the journey itself, you become more resilient (the YANGA effect again) and open to new opportunities which could lead to unexpected success.

As you start to think how your actions nourish growth ambitions, remember that the path to success is not linear. It's a series of actions, adjustments, and improvements, so enjoy the journey and celebrate small wins along the way.

Before we go into the next section, I want to cover three important points:

1. When you are positively energised, action will be easier to take. You'll be able to reframe your thinking from daily disappointment to steady growth.
2. Taking action to change your energy helps you create clarity about yourself and your own potential.
3. Think about what energises you, then bring more of it into your world every day. Consider the actions you want to take, starting today.

EMBRACING STABILITY AMIDST THE CHAOS OF CHANGE

There are three certainties in life:

- We all come into the world with nothing,
- We all die one day with nothing, and
- Today's world has uncertainty in abundance.

Just watch the news and you will see entire economies shift overnight. Action helps us navigate uncertainty, which is a form of empowerment. We can't control the external circumstances causing uncertainty, but we *can* control our response and how we move forward. Those who take action develop a sense of readiness and adaptability that allows them to navigate change more easily, positively, and effectively. Their mindset is one of looking forward and feeling confident versus being paralysed by the unknown.

ACTION BUILDS UP STRENGTH AND RESILIENCE

The more action you take, the more resilient you become. Each challenge faced and obstacle overcome strengthens your ability to 'bounce forward'. You don't want to bounce back to where you were; it's all about taking steps forward, even in a volatile difficult time. Bouncing forward in a volatile time means we need to think clearly, which means we must have a decluttered mind. Decluttering your mind has both physical and mental benefits, as it improves your overall wellbeing, leading to increased focus, reduced stress, and a greater sense of control and peace. You'll have reduced distractions, improved memory, enhanced decision-making abilities, and a greater sense of control.

Here are some practical tips to help you declutter by letting go of items that no longer serve a purpose:

- Organise your thoughts by journalling and mind-mapping.
- Seek help. Use mentors, a coach, or anyone else who can assist you. Life is busy, so things won't change overnight. With so many distractions, we all end up overthinking and find it difficult to be present in the moment.
- Honour how you feel and organise your thoughts to feel more calm and relaxed. When you write things down, you slow down and you can let go of any negative thoughts and emotions. Walk around if necessary, indoors or outdoors, whatever works for you. When you walk, you think differently.

A great reference here is a 2022 YouTube video titled *Find Mental Clarity and Declutter Your Mind: Mental Minimalism*, by Connie Reit. Remember, 'There is only one way to learn is through action. Everything you need to know you have learned through your journey.'

IT ONLY TAKES 12 MINUTES A DAY TO FOCUS

Now, I want you to do a simple exercise.

- Find 12 minutes (that's only 30 seconds every hour). Yes, that's *12 minutes per day* to think quietly about what you need to achieve your ambitions. If you can't find a straight 12 minutes, find two six-minute slots…but do it.
- Write down when you can do this, then block it out in your diary. In those 12 minutes, write down your responses to the following seven questions.
    - What do you see more clearly now?
    - What excuses have you always used for not achieving your ambitions?
    - What is the biggest change you are willing to make this week, starting today?
    - What change in your thinking would help you achieve your goals and ambitions faster and in a way you enjoy?
    - What, and whom, are you making important?

Go ahead, do the hard thinking and build your mental muscle. You only need 12 minutes per day of deep thoughtful consideration and enhance your problem-solving abilities.

BOUNCE FORWARD, NOT BACK, TO EMBRACE GROWTH

When individuals feel empowered to act, their stress levels often decrease. A January 2016 study published in the *Journal of Personality and Social Psychology* found that proactive individuals experience lower levels of stress and a greater sense of life satisfaction.

- Learning from experience. Each action you take provides feedback, whether positive or negative. Take this feedback as a gift, reflect on it, and enhance your learning and adaptability.
- Building resilience. Taking action in the face of adversity builds resilience. Research by psychologists including Martin Seligman shows that actively confronting challenges contributes to emotional resilience, enabling individuals to bounce back. However, I would say it's all about bouncing forward from setbacks more effectively.
- Taking action often involves collaboration and communication with others, which can strengthen social bonds. (More often, it is about building better social connections.) Strong social support networks are linked to improved mental health and enhanced problem-solving capabilities. Taking action becomes a fundamental strategy for personal development and critical problem management.

CONCLUSION

I will leave you with three strategies to take more effective action:

1. **Set clear small goals.** Break down larger goals into smaller actionable steps. Focus on what you can do today.
2. **Be accountable.** Build systems that hold you accountable for taking consistent action.
3. **Celebrate *action*, not just results.** Reward yourself for taking action regardless of the outcome. Celebrate efforts, not just success.

'TOUGH LOVE' MESSAGE

1. **Only you are stopping your actions today.** Nothing else is stopping you from turning a corner and doing something different today, developing a new idea, making something new happen. The only thing stopping you, in fact, is you and the choices you make.
2. **The world rewards those who act…so act.** It's not about having the perfect plan. If you strive for perfection or wait for the ideal moment, you'll endure 'energy-drainers' and disappointments along the journey. Instead, it's about doing things, learning, and evolving. Success, growth, and progress are reserved for those who are willing to step forward and take a chance. In the end, it is better to have tried and failed than to never have tried at all.

3. **Immediately step away from those energy-drainers.** Go back to the exercise where you put down the energy-drainers. What can you do to reduce these and do something about it today?

Start by becoming comfortable in the uncomfortable space by taking actions you've been holding back for weeks, months, or maybe even years. It doesn't matter if you are in your 20s, 30s, 40s, 50s or higher…it is never too late to start.

Once you have clarity of action, you'll be faced with many choices. Some will be very tough, but you'll be able to take the right step.

CHAPTER 4

EMBRACE HARD TIMES: ADVERSITY REWIRES OUR BRAIN

'THE WORLD BREAKS EVERYONE AND AFTERWARD SOME ARE STRONGER AT THE BROKEN PLACES.'

—ERNEST HEMINGWAY

Choices are fundamental to progress, shaping our paths and enabling personal growth while fostering a sense of urgency in our lives.

Making a choice is essential for several reasons, described by the **'DEAL'** effect:

1. **Direction:** Choices provide a sense of direction and purpose. They help us outline our goals and determine the steps needed to achieve them, guiding our actions.
2. **Empowerment:** The act of making a choice empowers us. It fosters a sense of control over our lives, boosting confidence and encouraging us to take initiative.
3. **Adaptability:** As life is full of uncertainties, making choices allows us to adapt to changing circumstances. It enables us to respond effectively to challenges and seize new opportunities.
4. **Learning:** Each choice carries the potential for learning. Regardless of the outcome, we gain valuable insights that help us grow and make better decisions in the future.

NOURISHING YOUR BRAIN EMPOWERS BETTER CHOICES

I would now like to talk about how nourishing your brain for growth enables you to make better choices and achieve positive action. Your actions nourish your mind and body, with those you perform during your darkest days more nourishing than the ones performed during the brightest days when everything's feeling perfect—it's true!

During those perfect days, when most of us feel that everything's amazing, our brains are nourished more than at any other time. After all, you're feeling like you could jump over the moon and everything's going right.

So, how can the dark days nourish our brains?

Usually, the darkest days feel draining, sucking the energy out of us. Often, we feel like we cannot cope, or don't want to deal with our issues and challenges any longer. Nourishing your brain is not about perfection; it's about balance and intentionality. When you prioritise brain health, you lay the foundations for meaningful growth and positive action. You create space for clarity, creativity, and courage to pursue your goals and move forward.

As you start to shift away from brain-drainers, you'll notice a profound shift in how you think and live. The energy you gain can be channelled into everything that matters most to you, from building relationships to pursuing your passions. Passion comes from suffering—again, it's true. When you have suffered and overcome some of the worst days, your passion to succeed and achieve becomes even stronger. Your brain and body can be thoroughly nourished when you manage a bad day.

Just think about a time when you've lived through one of your worst days ever.

- How did you overcome it?
- How did you come out on the other side?
- How did you feel once you overcame that challenge?

You felt good, right? No matter what we have experienced, even when we think it's the worst day ever and we have suffered the most, remember there are others who have experienced worse things than us.

EMBRACING THE UNPREDICTABLE, NAVIGATING UNEXPECTED FATE AND UNCERTAINTY

Now, imagine when my family heard back in March 1970 about my father's tragic car crash. That was no doubt a bad day (probably the worst they have faced). Often people say, 'Is it really *that* bad? Has anyone died?'. Well, in this instance, yes, someone did die—my father.

Now imagine what happened in the minds of my grandfather, my mother, my grandmother, my father's siblings. Did they feel nourished at that time? Probably not. They felt as if their world had ended. Yet their world didn't end. They still had to live it, and continue for the next generation.

Back in those days, most men in Asian families kept their feelings inside. They didn't share how they felt, as it was not the done thing in that era; instead, it was often seen as a sign of weakness. You had to show strength and courage, keeping your feelings deep inside.

At the same time, dealing with this tragic situation helped my family get to a better place where they could create opportunities and possibilities that they had not previously considered. It was a hard time, one when their collective brainpower was drained with negative thoughts and feelings of helplessness. Trying to find what they were grateful for at that moment was probably the most difficult thing to do.

Finding perspective must have seemed incredibly hard, but my grandfather took the high ground. He led, took control, and took action. He looked into the future to visualise how he could lead our family out of this terrible situation. This hard time became a growth engine—an energy-booster, you could say—for my grandfather. He climbed out of his valley of darkness, using the situation to realise my father's ambitions for his family. He was a true leader who had suffered more than any ordinary person.

THE SILENT STRUGGLE, THE WEIGHT OF UNSHARED EMOTIONS

Life happened in March 1970, yet no one wanted to open up about the deep sadness they were feeling—my understanding was that there were many silent moments. They kept everything inside, suppressing their anger, disappointment, and hurt, which eventually catches up with you in life. Not sharing emotions and feelings was in our blood; we didn't really talk about things, and that's what permeated through my mind.

From a very young age, I didn't really talk about my problems, my challenges, or any of the situations I experienced. I kept it all to myself, not really wanting to bother anyone about it.

I thought they had been through enough already, and wasn't really sure how to talk about my problems, or with whom.

WE DISCOVER MEANING THROUGH LIFE'S CHALLENGES

My father's death sparked a fire in my grandfather's belly to fuel our future by starting a new life. The happy life he had built in Nairobi had come to an abrupt end, but at the same time, the situation made a hero out of my grandfather in the way he endured and navigated the hurt in his heart. At only 10 months old, I didn't realise until much later how much sadness, anger, and hatred of the world I held as I grew up.

As a child, I was encouraged to keep my feelings deep inside and not share them, even in the darkest days. I often wonder why I wasn't able to talk about my feelings and emotions with anyone, but realised many years after that my dark days were no comparison to those of March 1970. Seriously, what could compare to that life-changing event? My dark days were probably insignificant in comparison.

During our biggest trials, we find our greatest strength. These experiences make us better, bringing people together and driving us to overcome challenges and seek out opportunities. While I hate thinking about my father's death as an opportunity, I probably wouldn't have had the strong relationship I formed with my grandparents, especially my grandfather, if he hadn't died then. Had my father been around, my grandfather would have settled back in India and we would have had a more distant relationship. Of course, I wanted my father around. (Who doesn't?) But our lives would've been very different, something I think about all the time.

NURTURING OUR MIND, A POWERFUL AND RESOURCEFUL TOOL

Our brains are truly remarkable. The brain works tirelessly to orchestrate every thought, emotion, and action. However, like any high-powered machine, it requires the right fuel, care, and conditions to operate at its best. When nourished properly, our brain becomes a powerful catalyst for personal growth and positive action. On the other hand, neglecting its needs can lead to mental fatigue, low progress, stress, diminished decision-making abilities, poor choices, anger, and irritation.

Every moment in life can lead to a brain energy drainer or a booster. Deciding which of these it will be depends on how you view and feel about these situations.

So, how can you make better-informed decisions and choices through the art of reflection?

Try this simple exercise.

1. Take the time to reflect, allowing you to clarify your goals, priorities, and intentions. This clarity helps reduce distractions as you become more aware of what truly matters and can focus your energy on those areas.
2. Regularly reflect and enhance self-awareness. This will help you recognise your thoughts, feelings, and behaviours. Understanding what energises or drains you can assist in making better choices.
3. Take time to think about your experiences and evaluate your options, as this will enable you make better-informed decisions. This will lead to greater confidence in your choices, reducing the tendency to second-guess yourself.
4. Reignite your motivation by celebrating small wins during your reflection time, as this will provide a sense of accomplishment.
5. Taking a few minutes for reflection can serve as a mental reset, helping your brain recharge while alleviating stress and anxiety.
6. Reflecting on challenges and how you've overcome them can strengthen your resilience. This mindset helps you bounce forward.

Your brain consumes an astonishing amount of energy—about 20% of your body's total supply, despite accounting for only 2% of its weight. This energy fuels everything from your ability to problem-solve to managing your emotions. When properly nourished, your brain functions efficiently, enabling you to:

- make clear decisions, reduce impulsive reactions, and enable rational thinking.
- remain motivated, as your energy reserves maintain resiliency against procrastination and fatigue.
- adapt and grow, becoming more flexible and capable of learning to overcome challenges.

ENERGISING THE MIND, REDUCING DRAINERS AND MAXIMISING BOOSTERS FOR OPTIMAL BRAIN HEALTH

It is important for you to prioritise your brain health—because no one else will.

You've got to nourish your brain. Physical issues start from your brain—that's a fact. Fuel your brain with the right energy-boosters and remove or drastically reduce those energy-drainers so that your brain can feel nourished and fresh as you make the right choices.

Create habits around your goals that nourish your brain health. Be consistent with your actions. The power of action leads to progress towards achieving your goals, accelerating your personal development, and manifesting your happiness. I can't guarantee you won't experience dark days in the future, but when you do, be strong and don't overthink things. It's wasted energy.

Find the right mentors or coaches who can guide you and provide the positive mental energy you need to get through tough times. The important thing is not to give up or overthink what others might say, or how they might react and respond to the outcomes of your actions.

Overthinking can significantly hinder action and progress for many reasons. Let me share five important impacts of overthinking with you:

- **Paralysis by analysis.** When you overthink, you often get caught up in a cycle of analysing every possible option and outcome. This can lead to decision paralysis, where the fear of making a wrong choice prevents any action from being taken.
- **Increased anxiety.** Overthinking can amplify your feelings of anxiety and worry. Constantly ruminating on potential problems or negative outcomes can create a sense of dread, making it difficult to take steps forward.
- **Fear of failure.** Overthinkers often dwell on the possibility of failure, which can create a sense of perfectionism. The fear of not meeting their own or others' expectations can prevent them from taking the necessary risks to move forward.
- **Loss of clarity.** Engaging in excessive thinking can cloud judgement—you suffer from 'brain fog', making it difficult to see the bigger picture. This lack of clarity can lead to confusion about what actions you need to take.
- **Negative self-talk.** Overthinking often involves negative self-talk where individuals criticise themselves for past

decisions or worry about future ones. This mindset can erode self-confidence and create a belief that taking action is futile or risky.

We are living in a fast-paced world where our responsibilities seem to be increasing, people want more of our time, and work pressure is becoming unmanageable. To manage day to day, we need to nourish our brains, make clear decisions, avoid procrastination, and take immediate action, whilst remaining energised to keep moving forward.

Here is a simple technique that I use pretty much every day, week, and month when I have to make some important decisions. It's the two-minute rule, an effective exercise to combat procrastination in decision making. Here's how it works.

- **Identify the decision.** Write down the decision you need to make. It could be anything from choosing what to eat for dinner to deciding on a project at work.
- **Set a timer.** Allocate just two minutes to think about the decision, setting a timer to keep yourself accountable.
- **List options.** In those two minutes, jot down any options or ideas related to the decision. Don't overthink; instead, just write down whatever comes to mind.
- **Evaluate quickly.** After the timer goes off, take a quick look at your list. Identify which options feel most reasonable or appealing.
- **Make a choice.** Choose one option and commit to it. If it's a minor decision, go ahead and take action immediately.

- **Reflect.** After you've made the decision, take a moment to reflect on the process.

The key to this exercise is to trust your instincts and make decisions more efficiently.

It's not easy to make the right choice, even the simpler ones, like 'What are we going to have for dinner tonight?'. That can turn into a complex problem, especially as we are all navigating through a very busy life schedule. However, think of your brain as a car. Your car will run smoothly until it needs some attention (i.e. it needs the right fuel, as well as frequent servicing). Your brain needs the same things. What you put into your brain—noise, clutter, or distractions—is down to you and no one else.

THE HIDDEN MENTAL COST OF POOR NUTRITION

While I'm not going to go into nutrition and the benefits of good nutrition in this book, consider the amount of sugar you put into your body. Sugar generally makes you feel tired. When you physically feel tired, you become mentally exhausted. There's a direct link between the two.

So, it's crucial to detox your brain and reduce the clutter. Consider the overwhelming noise from social media, which drains a tremendous amount of energy. Constantly experiencing FOMO (fear of missing out) is detrimental to your mental wellbeing. There's more to life than mindlessly scrolling and viewing others' curated online personas.

Studies show that persistent screen time, especially on mobile devices, negatively impacts decision-making and causes significant brain fatigue. If you currently spend three hours per day on social media, try reducing that to two hours. Use this freed-up time to read, take a walk, and truly experience the world around you. There's a universe of opportunity beyond the confines of social media—so go and explore it.

For an even bolder challenge, abstain from social media altogether for seven days. Document your observations—you'll see the world differently and feel exponentially better.

COURAGEOUS CHOICES, BEING BOLD, AND PUTTING YOURSELF FIRST

Carve out 20 minutes each day for self-care and personal growth, reducing your consumption of social media. Are you ready to do this? If you are, write it down. If you are not, ask yourself why. That way, you'll commit.

- **Step one is to schedule your time.** Choose a specific time each day that works for you, e.g. morning, lunch

break, or evening. Write it down in your calendar or set a daily reminder on your phone.
- **Step two is to create a list of activities.** Make a list of activities that you enjoy or that help you recharge—for example, reading a book or listening to a podcast, going for a walk or doing a short workout, practising mindfulness or meditation, journaling or doodling, engaging in a hobby (e.g. painting, cooking, or gardening), whatever you'd like.
- **Step three is to choose your activity.** Each day, select one activity from your list to focus on during your allocated 20 minutes.

CONCLUSION

This chapter is all about making choices. During our biggest trials, on those dark days, we sometimes make the best choices…but in order to make these, learn from those experiences, and move forward, good brain health is essential. Your brain needs to feel nourished. If you're emotionally imbalanced, or feeling fatigued, anxious, or stressed, you will not make the best decisions.

'TOUGH LOVE' MESSAGE

- Whatever situation you are facing, you have to make a choice—that's for real.

- Which way you go, and the outcome, will depend on the choices you make.
- You own your decisions and choices; no one else does.

What's stopping you from making clear decisions right now? And what's the one thing you can do right now to help you make that decision?

Own it. Make the choice.

This leads us to taking ownership and accountability, and how we deal with other people's opinions.

CHAPTER 5

SEEDS OF GROWTH: CHILDHOOD EXPERIENCES SHAPE OUR MINDSET

'THE MIND IS EVERYTHING. WHAT YOU THINK, YOU BECOME.'

—BUDDHA

When two people look at a problem or a challenge or an opportunity, they see the same thing with a different perspective. Our perspectives are formed from childhood, and eventually from our life experiences. But how much do our childhood experiences influence our minds as we grow up? Our perspective is up to us—we can choose to see things negatively, positively, or in a balanced way.

I have failed on many occasions, and both disappointed and delighted many people—some would describe me as an emotional human rollercoaster. I tried to please too many people too often, which definitely didn't work. Was I a people-pleaser? Maybe I was, but I'm not one today. Failure is an inevitable part of life, but why is it difficult to accept? Why is it so hard for *others* to accept? Next time you experience failure or make an unpopular decision, remember: It is not a reflection of your worth, but rather an opportunity to learn, grow, and ultimately succeed.

THE FORMATIVE POWER OF EARLY EXPERIENCES IN SHAPING IDENTITY

During our formative years, experiences, relationships, and environments play a pivotal role in shaping our values, beliefs and behaviours.

The concept of a growth mindset, popularised by psychologist Carol Dweck, revolves around the belief that abilities and intelligence can be developed through dedication and hard work. This chapter explores how our early experiences shape our mindsets and ultimately influence our professional journeys. As we navigate through these early experiences, we form attachments, learn about the world, and begin to establish our identity, which continues to evolve throughout our lives.

As a child, I encountered a myriad of experiences that shaped my beliefs about myself, my family, my community, and the world around me and beyond. At the time I was born, who could have foreseen the drastic turn my life would take by just 10 months old? Instead of the normal upbringing, with a father to guide and catch me when I fall, I would forge a different path—one without that irreplaceable dad to guide me, to offer a comforting embrace when feeling blue or lost, or to simply sit beside me in companiable silence. We all need that father figure, that pillar of strength and protection in our lives.

My grandfather became my father figure. He was there, solid and reliable, occupying that role of protector and guide. We'd watch cricket together or just sit quietly, enjoying each other's company. He played an important role in taming my fiery teen spirit, and if it wasn't for his calm manner and influence I would be quite a different character today. My father was with me in my heart, becoming the inner voice guiding my life.

THE IMPORTANCE OF PRAISE AND CELEBRATING SMALL WINS IN PERSONAL GROWTH

Whether it's the encouragement or discouragement of a teacher, the harsh criticism of a parent or grandparent, or the camaraderie of friends, each interaction leaves an imprint in our mind.

Growing up, victories large and small went uncelebrated until my 1990 and 1992 graduations—the milestones my grandfather deemed worthy of true celebration. What I've realised along the way, and now as a father of three wonderful loving children, is that children praised for their simple efforts (completing a challenging puzzle, for example) are more likely to embrace challenges later in life. They learn that struggle is part of learning and that persistence can lead to success. Conversely, a child who is only recognised for their innate talent may come to fear failure, believing that their worth is tied to their abilities rather than their efforts.

I recall one year when I was 12, at the start of high school and after years of being told I was not good enough, I suddenly had the drive to show my family I could achieve decent marks and not the usual 30% or 40% C and D grades, which were always disappointing. Towards the end of that year, I worked really hard and took home an 80% grade in English language, which was a proud moment for me. I ran home, smiling all the way and running away from those school bullies, and waited until my grandfather, GR, returned home from work at 6:00 pm. We had a disciplined 6:00 to 6:30 pm dinner time, and GR expected everyone to be at the dining table ready to eat. If you were late, he would keep everyone waiting until all seats were full.

This was my moment, a place where I could show everyone I was smarter than they thought. I waited for the right moment, as every day we would be asked what we did at school and what we learned. When my turn came, I had the paper as proof—a big 80% in red in the top right-hand corner of the page of my English language essay. I was expecting my good news to spread like wildfire around the table and beyond. I heard 'Well done', we paused, and then the question: 'Was it the top mark in the class?'.

The negative impact of this conversation lasted a long time. Over the next few months, I went back to below 50% as I didn't see the point of doing any better as no one really cared unless I scored 90% plus, which in my mind would never happen. I didn't bother sharing any good results and no one really asked any further questions. I blamed everyone else for the way I felt, which was wrong of me; I didn't realise it back then, though, as my reaction and response to the challenge was really my own responsibility. During that dinner, I was thrown a 'stretch challenge' but felt I was being punished.

I was driven to show others how good I was, but what I should have done was work hard for *me*. Trying to achieve better scores for others simply affected my mental wellbeing. (I was angry and frustrated, becoming rebellious.) I realised this long after leaving high school. All I ever wanted was to be met with a reassuring, 'That's okay, you'll get better with practice' every time I failed or didn't quite hit the mark.

EMPOWERMENT THROUGH RESILIENCE – THE ART OF PICKING YOURSELF UP

Growing up, I faced immense challenges yet refused to give up. I kept moving forward, making marginal gains. My grandfather pushed me to do better, stretching my thinking and abilities. However, his actions inadvertently instilled a fear of failure in me.

As a teen, I launched many ideas and money-making initiatives, but kept failing. This fear of failure became a mental block, preventing the success I desired. That said, some initiatives did work—I had a knack for sales, quickly building strong teams in network marketing. Earning good money, I surprised my family with cash at home instead of a traditional job.

Yet something felt off about the high-pressure sales culture. Eventually, I chose a safe career path my grandfather would approve of—joining a bank's prestigious graduate program, just like my father and grandfather before me. When I informed my grandfather on his birthday, his proud embrace meant more than all the cash I'd made.

THE IMPACT OF CHILDHOOD EXPERIENCES CANNOT BE OVERSTATED

When I was younger, many people made fun of me for being, as they say, 'thick' because of my poor grades and playful attitude. Maybe people around me didn't want to feel embarrassed by my questions, so asked me to leave the room. I felt the constant flow of comments criticising my brainpower (or lack thereof) and playful attitude stifling my creativity. For example, I loved drawing and painting, but was discouraged from following these passions because they were not seen as a proper career. Who knows what I could have done had I pursued my passion.

Our early experiences serve as a blueprint that influences the choices we make throughout our lives. Positive experiences foster confidence and open-mindedness, while negative experiences can lead to fear or hesitation in certain situations. Understanding how these formative years shape our preferences, values, and coping mechanisms allows us to recognise patterns in our choices and empowers us to make intentional decisions that align with our true selves.

The journey towards a growth mindset begins with self-awareness. Recognising fixed beliefs, those that suggest our abilities are static, is the first step. It's essential to challenge these beliefs by reframing our thoughts. So, instead of saying, 'I'm not good at this', we can say, 'I'm not good at this *yet*.' Or 'You are not good at that' can become 'You will become better at that.' This simple shift in language opens the door to multiple possibilities.

As my story illustrates, our experiences influence who we are and our behaviour, but they do not define us. I broke every rule under the sun when I was at high school and as a teenager; whatever I was told not to do, I did. I was simply curious, wanting to see what the big deal was when I was told not to smoke, drink, get into fights, stay out late at night and go clubbing, talk to girls (most strict Hindu families had this rule for their boys), or eat meat (especially beef, as cows are a sacred animal in Hindu culture). I did everything, and for a long time enjoyed it. I recall the day I had my first Big Mac—and boy, I *loved* the feeling that I was breaking a sacred rule and no one knew I had done it.

Eventually, though, something changed inside me. It was those deep reflections within, connecting with my father, my inner thoughts, and my drive to show my family and the world that I could achieve success, that helped me turn a corner.

THE SEEDS OF GROWTH, RESILIENCE, AND CURIOSITY CAN BE PLANTED THROUGHOUT OUR LIVES

We can transform past and present experiences into opportunities for growth, innovation, and fulfilment. We nurture our very essence and potential. Understand your inner power, because you alone control your mindset.

Today, a resilient mindset is critical. The world is changing at a breakneck pace, with generational shifts driving continuous upheaval. These challenges can feel overwhelming.

However, those who adopt a resilient, action-oriented mindset are uniquely equipped to navigate this landscape, turning obstacles into opportunities and uncertainty into innovation.

Consider how you grapple with rapid technological advancements, including AI. If you possess a growth (i.e. a more resilient) mindset, you will likely view these changes as opportunities for innovation rather than threats to stability. You invest in upskilling, encourage creative problem-solving, and promote a culture of continuous learning. By contrast, those with a fixed (more negative) mindset may resist change, clinging to outdated practices and risking obsolescence.

NOURISHING THE BODY ENHANCES THE MIND FOR SUSTAINED SUCCESS

In addition to nurturing a growth mindset, nourishing our brains with energy-boosters is essential for sustaining our success. The human brain is a remarkable organ, constantly processing information and adapting to new situations.

When I was younger I (like many other children) was encouraged to eat my greens, more fruit and healthy foods—often those which I didn't particularly like. I was also encouraged to do more exercise, but all these things we are told to do we often don't, going the opposite way instead. My grandfather very rarely ate out, always wanting nutritious home-cooked meals, but I loved eating out and going to the local fish and chips shop even after having a meal at home. Although I believe I did eat healthily in my formative years, I could have done more to stimulate my physical and mental health, that's for sure.

Nutrition plays a significant role in brain health. Foods rich in omega-3 fatty acids, antioxidants, and vitamins can enhance cognitive function and improve mood. A diet that supports brain health can bolster our ability to think creatively, make sound decisions, and respond effectively to work and personal challenges.

I now exercise for up to an hour every single day. When I miss a day, I feel I haven't actually lived well that day—it's a habit which increases blood flow to the brain, which promotes the growth and survival of neurons. This not only enhances cognitive function, but also reduces stress and anxiety, providing a mental buffer against the chaos of a rapidly changing environment. The endorphins released during physical activity can also boost your mood, making it easier to maintain a positive outlook, which is essential for cultivating a growth mindset.

THE VITAL ROLE OF SLEEP IN PROMOTING BRAIN HEALTH

As a child I always found ways to stay up late, taking a torch with me so I could read a comic when the lights were out. I didn't realise how much of an impact sleep had on the way I thought, acted, and performed the next day. During sleep, the brain undergoes a process that supports memory consolidation and emotional regulation. Adequate rest allows for the removal of toxins that accumulate during the time we are awake. Sleep is therefore a fundamental pillar for sustained brain health. Prioritising sleep allows us to recharge, making us better equipped to face the challenges that lie ahead.

Going back to 1993, when I joined a highly regarded bank on their renowned graduate management program, we lived by the 'Work hard, play hard' mantra. We spent many long hours into the late evenings working and studying for higher qualifications, and then often went out for a few drinks that turned into a few more…and the next thing I knew, I was strolling in at 2:00 a.m. or 3:00 a.m., then getting up again at 7:00 a.m. to get into the plush city offices. This went on for months, but I had the energy as a young man, believing that I could continue performing at my best with three to four hours of sleep every night (or most nights).

Nope, I couldn't do it. It all caught up with me eventually. It was 1994, about 18 months into my new job, when I read about how a good night's sleep recharges your brain's energy more than anything else. The thing is, my grandfather used to say the same thing: 'Always get a good night's sleep; sleep early and you will feel better for it.' I should have listened to him then; his words are there in my subconscious mind, guiding me along. I feel GR and RG are talking together, sending me the right signals and ensuring I always land on my feet, whatever the challenge.

Nowadays, I could have had the worst day ever, dealing with multiple problems, challenges, and issues, but instead I sleep peacefully for 7 to 8 hours every night. I've created the habit and conditioned my mind. With a peaceful night's sleep, I'm then ready to face the day, bouncing forward and getting on with what I have to do.

Scientific evidence shows the importance of a good night's sleep:

- **Mental fatigue:** Lack of sleep is linked to increased mental fatigue. Research published in *Neuropsychology* (2016) indicates that sleep deprivation can lead to significant declines in mental energy and motivation. This can result in feelings of tiredness and decreased efficiency in mental tasks.
- **Emotional regulation:** Sleep is essential for emotional stability. A 2023 study in *JAMA Psychiatry* found that individuals who are sleep deprived are more prone to mood disturbances and negative emotions. Conversely, good-quality sleep has been associated with higher levels of happiness and emotional wellbeing.
- **Memory consolidation:** Sleep is vital for memory consolidation, which affects learning and information retention. Research in the journal *Nature* (2021) shows that sleep helps to strengthen neural connections that form memories, thus improving clarity of thinking and recall.
- **Overall wellbeing:** According to the National Sleep Foundation, good sleep is not only crucial for cognitive performance, but also contributes to overall physical and mental health, influencing happiness and life satisfaction. So, a good night's sleep is essential for maintaining mental clarity, reducing fatigue, and enhancing our overall happiness.

You may be tempted to dismiss this as mere platitudes, but I urge you to try it for yourself. Experiment and discover what works best to help you refocus and reframe your mindset. The rewards are immeasurable. My daily gym sessions have become a cherished refuge from the noise and distractions, a space to commune with RG and my true, centred self, as well as to stay disciplined. This is the power of prioritising your health and happiness. You can find something similar that works for you, and I guarantee—once you create the habit, you'll never look back.

Before we conclude the chapter, I want to share a little exercise that will help you unpack your childhood learnings, impacts, and outcomes:

1. **Create the framework.** Draw a simple table with three columns labelled as follows: Childhood Learning, Failure or Challenge; Impact; Outcome.
2. **Identify learning, failures or challenges.** Think about childhood experiences. Write down up to five specific failures or challenges in the first column.
3. **Reflect on impact.** For each failure and challenge, consider its impacts. How did this failure affect you? Did it affect others? How? What were the immediate consequences? Write these reflections in the second column.
4. **Analyse outcomes.** Now think about the outcomes. What were the long-term effects of this learning, failure or

challenge? Did you learn anything from the experience? How did it shape your future actions or decisions? How does it affect your decisions and choices today? Document your thoughts in the third column.

5. **Review and reflect.** Once you've filled in the table, take a moment to review what you've written. Reflect on the following questions: What patterns do you notice in your learnings, failures? Are these insightful? Did you learn anything new about yourself? How can you use these insights to improve in the future?

As I get better at sharing personal experiences, I'm now going to share a couple of real examples that have impacted me:

	Learning/ Failure	**Impact**	**Outcome**
Story 1	Not doing my homework on time (or at all).	Disappointed teachers, poor grades, letters sent home and lost learning time.	Understood the importance of meeting deadlines and getting things done.
Story 2	Arguing with family.	Strained relationships.	Learned the importance of communication and listening.

By completing this exercise, you will gain valuable insights into how your childhood learnings and failures can lead to growth and improvement.

CONCLUSION

Childhood is the seed of growth, profoundly shaping our choices and behaviours throughout life. Formative experiences mould our perceptions, values, and coping mechanisms, laying the groundwork for our response to challenges.

By understanding this lasting impact, we can cultivate self-awareness and resilience, making conscious choices aligned with our true selves. Embracing childhood's lessons empowers us to face obstacles with confidence and adaptability, guiding us towards personal growth and fulfilment.

A growth mindset that can deal with a forever-changing, high-pressure, and chaotic world demands a multifaceted approach. At the end of this chapter, I leave you with these three important 'tough love' messages:

- Your childhood plants seeds for your growth mindset, so use your early year experiences to empower yourself, embrace challenges, and learn from them.
- Celebrate the small wins and reward yourself for marginal gains through the process. It is not always about the big wins—every win counts.
- Nourish your brain with energy-boosters, equipping you with the cognitive and emotional resources necessary to navigate complexity and ambiguity. So, don't just go for convenience. Instead, eat healthily, get a good night's sleep, and surround yourself with positive influences.

In this dynamic landscape, the commitment to learning, resilience and wellbeing becomes not just beneficial, but essential for you to thrive in our world of tomorrow. Your growth and success will come from planning, but planning *too* far ahead is a waste of time which will only lead to disappointment.

Instead, just focus on the next few steps on your ambitious path. After all, the world is moving at a *much* faster pace than you can plan for.

CHAPTER 6

PATH TO AMBITION: THINKING TOO FAR AHEAD DOESN'T WORK

'TO BE YOURSELF IN A WORLD THAT IS CONSTANTLY TRYING TO MAKE YOU SOMETHING ELSE IS THE GREATEST ACCOMPLISHMENT.'

—RALPH WALDO EMERSON

Ambition is a powerful force that drives us to pursue our dreams and reach for the stars. Achieving our ambitions requires focusing deeply on ourselves, understanding our desires, making informed choices, and cultivating the right mindset. This chapter will explore how homing in on your individual aspirations can lead to a fulfilling and successful life.

First and foremost, the journey begins with self-discovery. What do you genuinely want? This question may seem simple, yet many people struggle to answer it. To uncover your true ambitions, engage in introspection by reflecting on your passions, values, and interests. What activities make you lose track of time? What causes ignite a fire within you? By identifying what resonates with you, you create a roadmap for your ambitions. A foundation upon which to build your dreams.

HARNESSING EDUCATION'S TRANSFORMATIVE POWER TO REALISE AMBITION

I was always told that to be successful and achieve your ambitions, you must have a decent education—this was the Asian family way. Now, don't get me wrong here. I believe that education is very important, but higher education is not for everyone. We're all different. There are many examples of very successful people who dropped out of university or college to pursue their dreams—Bill Gates (co-founder of Microsoft), Steve Jobs (co-founder of Apple), Mark Zuckerberg (founder of Facebook), Richard Branson (founder of Virgin), and James Cameron (director of *Titanic* and *Avatar*), to name a few. They took a courageous decision and challenged conventional thinking and attitudes.

At one point, when I was in sixth form, I wanted to give it all up and get a job to start earning money. As my key career driver was financial reward, money was a real motivator for me to keep pursuing my dreams. This burning desire to earn more money and be successful came from my childhood, when money was scarce and times were hard. What we had, though, was an abundance of love in the household. This combination of very little money and an abundance of love drove me to consider earning more and providing my family with a better life. I wanted to do it for them.

So instead of really studying hard, my ambition at college was to earn more cash and provide for my family. There's nothing wrong with that, right? One conversation with my grandfather, who was my mentor and coach even though he didn't realise it, soon doused the 'Earn more money now' fire in my belly. He said, 'What will you do when you want to get a promotion and someone with better qualifications gets it because they're better educated?'. I knew then that I didn't want to be in that position. My grandfather had a razor-sharp focus; his driver was to achieve my father's ambition to give his children the best education.

TAKING THE LEAP: THE CALL TO ACTION FOR TURNING AMBITIONS INTO REALITY

Once you have clarity on your desires, take action. Ambition without action is just a wish. Achieving your vision may take time, but set short-term milestones to keep progressing.

I've long talked about writing a book, but work, home life, and others' discouragement always got in the way. Peeling back the excuses, I realized I was the one holding myself back. Now, at 55, the universe has aligned to empower me to write my first book.

It's essential to make the right choices—evaluating opportunities through the lens of your ambitions. Learn to say 'no' to distractions that don't serve your goals. For years, I was a people-pleaser, trying to make everyone happy at the expense of my own progress.

Your environment plays a huge role. If you're surrounded by people who want you to be who you were, cut those ties—or if this is not possible, reduce your interactions with these people. They'll only hold you back from achieving your ambitions.

NAVIGATING THE FINE LINE BETWEEN JOB SECURITY AND CALCULATED RISK

My ambition has always been to lead a successful business. I've taken a squiggly career path and worked for eight global organisations, successfully navigating my path to senior and executive levels, but somehow I never felt fulfilled. Even up until recently, somebody spoke to me about my career path and said, 'Well, you should have stayed with the bank. That was a secure job and you could have walked away with a lovely pension.' It's not what I wanted, and I also don't really need to hear what I should have done, could have been, or could have had.

Think about your own situation. Have you followed society or family expectations through your career? Or have you followed your heart and mind to pursue a career and personal growth path that you really wanted? So many times we do things because others want us to. It's time that you put yourself and your ambitions first, starting today.

To do this, it's really important to cultivate a positive and resilient mindset. With challenges inevitable on the path to achieving your ambitions, how you respond to these obstacles will determine your success.

- Embrace a forward-thinking mindset where setbacks are viewed as opportunities for learning and development.
- When faced with difficulties, remind yourself that every successful person has encountered failures and rejections along their way. I've lost count of how many failures I've encountered in my journey, and had fun learning along the way. Each one has taught me an important life lesson, boosting my innate ability to bounce forward.
- What sets successful people apart is their ability to persevere, adapt, and continue moving forward no matter what happens or how hard they fall. They may fall down, but they always get back up and keep moving forward.

RESILIENCE IN ACTION, PERSONAL JOURNEYS OF FAILURE, AND EMPOWERING LESSONS

Not being a superstar academic, I found A-Levels challenging. In fact, these were the hardest exams I have ever done. I was distracted with the get-rich-quick network marketing schemes; after all, my ambition at college was to make more cash for my family. The outcome—poor A-Level results—impacted my choice of university. I didn't make the grades, so all the universities that I applied for (and which had previously made me provisional offers) now rejected me. To avoid personal embarrassment and disappointing my family again, I went through the UK clearing system to get into the first business course I could. Having done this, I got into a higher national diploma Business and Finance program at Kingston University. That way, I could confidently say, 'I'm going to university,' which pleased my family. (I also didn't have to retake my A-Levels.) At the end of my Diploma in Business and Finance, I applied for a financial consultant position. In my mind, I was super-qualified and should be able to get this job. I did really well through the rigorous selection process, getting through to the final two. Unfortunately, they picked the other candidate who had a degree. I never wanted to be in that position again.

I once worked for a global financial service brand in a senior director role, overseeing 18 markets. I was living the high life, travelling the world in business class and staying at 5-star hotels. I thought I had reached the pinnacle of my career. Where I failed was not in my job, but with my family. Travelling was part and parcel of the work that I did. The extensive travel meant that I missed important dates—for example, school events, family socials, date nights, movie nights, and important time together. This is time I will never get back.

While running an advertising and PR business in the Middle East, I lost a major client. Being customer-focused, this really hurt me, especially when we could have recovered this so quickly and easily. We lost because I failed to check a crucial detail, assuming my team had checked it. But at the end of the day, I couldn't blame them. It was my responsibility to make sure all the details were correct when we were pitching for the business. When I say 'pitching', I mean that this was a contract renewal. Unfortunately, there were a number of errors in the main presentation, including spelling, grammar, and general facts and insights. Being very busy pursuing new business, I didn't have the time to check details. I don't really blame the clients, but boy, did this eat me up for a long period of time.

EMBRACING NEW PERSPECTIVES TO CONQUER LIFE'S MOST SIGNIFICANT CHALLENGES

I now want to introduce you to a small exercise that will help you rethink your approach to your ambitions and your goals. The objective is to shift your perspective on challenges by identifying potential opportunities they present, involving six key steps.

1. **Identify a challenge.** Write down a specific challenge you are currently facing, something that you need to deal with now or in the next 30 days (especially around achieving your ambitions and your goals). Be as detailed as possible about the situation.
2. **Explore the feelings.** Reflect on how this challenge makes you feel. Write down your emotions and thoughts associated with it.
3. **Ask key questions.** Consider the following questions to help reframe your challenge.

What skills or strengths can I develop by facing this challenge?	How might this challenge lead to new opportunities or experiences?	Are there alternative perspectives on this situation that could help me see this differently?	What can I learn from this challenge that could benefit me in the future?

4. **List opportunities.** Based on your reflections, create a list of potential opportunities that could arise from this challenge. Think about personal growth, new connections, or unexpected outcomes.
5. **Action plan.** Choose one opportunity from your list and write down actionable steps you can take to pursue it.
6. **Reflect.** This usually happens after a week or two. Revisit your exercise, reflecting on any changes in your perspective and the steps you took towards the opportunity.

This exercise helps cultivate a growth mindset, enabling you to see challenges as pathways to learning and development. Visualisation can also be a powerful tool in achieving your ambitions. Spend time imagining yourself living your dream life. What does it look like? How does it feel? By vividly picturing your goals, you reinforce your commitment to them and create a strong emotional connection to your aspirations.

GROWTH TAKES TIME; EACH STEP YOU TAKE IS PART OF YOUR UNIQUE JOURNEY

The journey toward ambition is linear. Celebrate your progress no matter how small, being kind to yourself during setbacks. Recognise that growth takes time and that each step you take is part of your unique journey. By fostering a compassionate relationship with yourself, you create a nurturing environment that supports your ambitions. I always say that a day without love and laughter is a day not worth living. We all have our challenges, some deeper than others, but a daily dose of love and laughter will help you overcome any setbacks—it's so important. Start by loving what you do and laughing at some of the things you've done or seen.

I often use my daily commute into London and back home after a long day to consider what I loved and what I could laugh about. I'm sure some of my 'fellow travellers' must have thought I was a bit crazy smiling at myself as I sat there thinking. But worrying about what others think is not my concern. If they thought I was a bit crazy, then great, that's their choice. How others respond to what you do is their choice and nothing to do with you.

Achieving your ambition starts with focusing on you and what you truly want in life. Through self-discovery, actionable steps, informed choices and a resilient mindset, you can transform your dreams into reality. If you try and achieve your ambitions for others, and by making everyone else around you happier, you'll get nowhere. (I speak from personal experience.) Remember, though the path may be challenging and may sometimes feel impossible, take one step at a time.

As you embark on this journey, trust in your ability to create the life you desire and let your ambitions guide you toward a future with purpose and fulfilment. I've realised what it takes to achieve ambition quite late in life. Though I'm not sure why, I feel I've been distracted. There's been a lot of noise and a lot of 'brain fog', which prevented me from thinking with clarity and purpose. It was only over the last 12 to 18 months that I gained absolute clarity regarding my purpose and where I want to go.

HARNESSING PAST EXPERIENCES TO PROPEL FUTURE ACHIEVEMENTS

My purpose is to inspire and improve lives. This came from reflecting on my family history and how they coped with adversity. Understanding your roots is the key to living a purposeful, fulfilling life.

Surrounding yourself with positive influences—people, environments, and experiences—creates an atmosphere that encourages growth. Supportive communities can motivate us, celebrate our wins, and guide us through challenges. They become our cheerleaders, reminding us of our worth.

In contrast, negative influences drain our energy, breed self-doubt, and stifle ambition. Fostering uplifting connections is crucial. Our heritage also provides wisdom, traditions, and stories to inform our present and future. Inspired by my ancestors' resilience, I found the courage to pursue my own dreams.

I'm proud to be part of my family. I hear my late father's voice through inner conversations that bring out my creativity, a connection which reminds me that I'm carrying the strength of those who came before.

Creating a positive environment isn't just about people, either, as nature too can refresh and invigorate. Long-term ambition is vital, but you must approach it with adaptability. Action is the catalyst that transforms ambition into reality.

Action is the engine that drives progress, but you need a plan:

1. **Importance of planning.** While ambition is crucial, it needs to be paired with a clear plan of action.

2. **Learning from action.** Although many people hesitate to act due to the fear of failure or uncertainty, taking action allows for experimentation and learning. Even if the initial steps don't lead to the desired outcome, they provide valuable insights that can inform our future actions and help us overcome fear.
3. **Action is necessary.** Recognising that action is a necessary part of the journey can help individuals push past any barriers.

Ambition is the fuel but action is the engine that drives progress. It's the *combination* of the two that leads to meaningful achievements.

ACKNOWLEDGING THE CRITICAL ROLE OF SELF-COMPASSION AND SELF-CARE IN REALISING YOUR AMBITIONS

Self-compassion plays a crucial role in achieving ambition, especially in the fast-paced modern world where external pressures can be overwhelming. Reduced self-criticism fosters resilience, enabling you to bounce forward and continue pursuing your goal. When you are compassionate towards yourself, you are more likely to stay motivated. You approach your goals with a sense of curiosity and enthusiasm rather than fear of judgement or failure. Self-compassion contributes to overall mental wellbeing, reducing stress and anxiety. A healthier mindset can enhance focus and clarity, making it easier to pursue goals effectively.

When I was much younger, the lack of self-compassion significantly hindered my ability to achieve goals and my ambitions. Overly critical of myself, I was paralysed by the fear of failure, which led to diminished motivation and productivity. I lived without the kindness of self-compassion and for years struggled to recover from challenges, which made it difficult to maintain resilience and pursue my ambitions with confidence. The absence of self-compassion stifled my creativity and limited the potential for success. I put on a 'go-getter' external presence, but deep inside I was suffering from negative self-doubt. This changed over time, as I started to understand the hardships my family overcame and surrounded myself with high-quality coaches who enabled me to open up and helped me unpack my own 'brain fog'. I wasn't always one to ask for help, but I'm glad I did.

CONCLUSION

Be true to yourself to pursue your dreams. Achieving a life you're genuinely proud of requires positivity and learning from your roots.

Cultivate supportive relationships, honour your ancestors, and create uplifting environments. This empowers you to chase your ambitions with confidence.

Embrace the lessons of the past while building positivity in the present. Navigate life's complexities with the strength inherited from your lineage and the respect of your community.

Nurture your journey to live with pride, purpose, and genuine happiness. Embrace your path, honour your roots, and let positivity illuminate the way to a fulfilled, proud existence.

MY 'TOUGH LOVE' MESSAGES TO YOU

Grab a pen and write down what you are willing to commit today towards achieving your ambition(s).

I commit to:

What is the one thing you will do differently starting now, in order to take that one step forward?

The one thing I will do:

If you don't make time to take steps forward, no one else will do it for you. Visualise your end goal. What does it look like? How does it feel?

You will inevitably face challenges and failures in pursuit of your ambitions. How do you pick yourself up and bounce forward in life?

CHAPTER 7

NOT EVERY SETBACK IS THE END OF THE STORY: PEOPLE RISE FROM PERSONAL FAILURES

'SUCCESS IS NOT FINAL, FAILURE IS NOT FATAL. IT IS THE COURAGE TO CONTINUE THAT COUNTS.'

—WINSTON CHURCHILL

Failure and mistakes are human; they don't make you insufficient. When faced with setbacks, learn to pivot, take small steps, and keep trying. Setbacks aren't the end, but stepping stones to new adventures.

To succeed, you must avoid becoming a victim. Resisting the urge to find someone to rescue you from 'persecutors' like life, the world, others' opinions. The only person who can get you out of a setback is YOU.

Embrace your missteps as opportunities for growth, not reasons to blame external factors. Own your journey, learn from slip-ups, and propel yourself forward. Setbacks are inevitable—but with the right mindset, they become catalysts for your next chapter in life.

EMBRACING SETBACKS, UNDERSTANDING THEIR EMOTIONAL IMPACT AND RECOGNISING THEIR CRUCIAL ROLE IN PERSONAL GROWTH

Setbacks can be disheartening, leaving us questioning our choices. Yet, what if we shifted our perspective? What if we saw these setbacks not as failures, but as unique opportunities for growth, learning, and adaptation, especially in the context of generational differences?

In this chapter, I'll share pivotal setbacks from the past five decades that have shaped my career and life. You'll see how I overcame genuine hardship and kept moving forward, rather than succumbing to a victim mentality and blaming external factors.

Setbacks are a universal human experience—whether stemming from personal failures, workplace challenges, or life changes. Recognizing them as catalysts for change, not just obstacles, is essential. Setbacks prompt self-reflection, pushing us to ask: What went wrong? What can I learn? How can I improve my approach for future success?

We must embrace the idea that our abilities and intelligence can be developed through dedication and hard work. Individuals with a growth mindset view challenges and setbacks as opportunities to improve rather than as reflections of their self-worth. Each setback can teach us something valuable, whether it's a new skill, a different approach, or a deeper understanding of ourselves and our motivations.

LEARNING FROM GENERATIONAL DIFFERENCES

In a world that is increasingly diverse, understanding generational differences can also be a significant factor in how we respond to setbacks. Each generation, be it the Baby Boomers, Generation X, Millennials, or Generation Z, brings its own perspectives, values, and ways of responding to challenges. For instance:

- Millennials and Gen Zs are often characterised by their ability to adapt and being tech-savvy.
- Baby Boomers may rely on traditional methods and a wealth of experience.

When a setback occurs in a workplace setting, these generational differences can lead to varied responses:

- A Millennial may quickly pivot to a digital solution.
- A Baby Boomer might prefer face-to-face communication and tried-and-tested methods.

THE DANGER OF OVERANALYSING SETBACKS AND THE JOURNEY TO DISCOVER THEIR ROOT CAUSES

When you experience a setback, you have to reframe, rethink, pivot, and move forward, at pace. I recall being in meetings in a number of the companies I worked for, back when I was in my thirties and forties, where we would overanalyse every issue that arose, every problem we encountered, every setback we faced. We had meeting after meeting after meeting, getting nowhere and wasting time. The long debates and discussions simply became boring.

The important thing is to get to the root cause of the issue:

- What caused the setback, and how can you overcome that going forward?
- What do you need to do next?
- What's the action plan?
- Who's going to do it and when?
- What support do you need to make it happen?

Reframe every setback into a real opportunity and not another problem. And if you're surrounded by people who keep bringing it back to a problem, it's time to cut ties and change the people around you.

TRANSFORMING SETBACKS INTO STEPPING STONES, REFRAMING CHALLENGES AS CATALYSTS FOR LEARNING

So, how do we reframe a bad situation to one that enables us to learn, grow, and develop, while nourishing our brains to seek opportunities? You must adjust your approach to new situations, especially when faced with setbacks. This is crucial for personal and professional development. The ability to adapt is often what separates those who thrive from those who are merely surviving.

Here are six key steps that will turn a setback to a real-life learning opportunity where you can thrive and revive.

- **Reflect:** Take time to analyse what happened. What were the contributing factors? What could have been done differently? Take the emotion out of it.
- **Seek facts:** Understand the impact, then move on.
- **Seek feedback:** Engage with others, particularly those from different generations who were involved or who understand the problem or setback you faced. Their

perspectives can offer you fresh insights that you may not have considered.
- **Set new goals:** Use your reflections and feedback to establish new, achievable goals. These should be informed by your setbacks and the lessons you've learned.
- **Embrace change:** Understand that change is a constant in life. Be open to adjusting your methods and approaches based on your experiences and the feedback you received. Remember, feedback is a gift. How you respond to feedback is entirely your choice. Use feedback in your reflections to help you bounce forward in a stronger way.
- **Cultivate resilience:** Building resilience is a key to navigating future setbacks. Focus on developing coping strategies that empower you to bounce forward stronger than ever.

I once obsessed over setbacks, letting this impact my mental health. The overthinking consumed me—I felt drained, stressed, anxious. But I soon realized that facing life's challenges, without the burden of anxiety, can lead to a healthier mindset and greater personal growth.

Here are a few reasons why it's highly beneficial to adopt this perspective.

- **Setbacks give you a perspective shift.** They are often temporary and may provide valuable lessons. View them as part of your journey.
- **Setbacks provide real growth opportunities.** Each setback can be a chance to learn and improve. By

focusing on what you can gain from the experience, you can enhance your skills, resilience, and ability to handle change and pressure.

- **Change is inevitable and constant.** In fact, it's not even *change* anymore—that's just normal life. Not worrying about setbacks reduces stress, while obsessing over them can increase stress and anxiety. So, stop worrying to improve your mental health and wellbeing.
- **Nothing is more important in life than your own mental wellbeing.** Overcoming setbacks fosters creativity. When you're not bogged down by the fear of failure, you can think more creatively and be more willing to take risks.
- **Experiencing setbacks can also help you strengthen relationships.** Sharing your setbacks with others can foster deeper connections and support networks. People are often willing to help, and discussing challenges can lead to valuable insight. Also, remember that these people may not necessarily be the ones who are closest to you.

When you overcome setbacks without excessive worry, you have the chance to inspire others. You can inspire everyone around you. Your resilience can serve as a powerful example, encouraging others to face their challenges with courage. I'm sharing my personal stories, both professional and personal, with you in this book to show you that you are not alone, and to instil some courage in you to take your next actions.

HOW PERSONAL STORIES CAN FOSTER GROWTH AND NAVIGATE BEYOND SETBACKS

Before I share some of my personal setbacks and experiences and explain how I overcame them, I want to take a step back and define what a setback is, offering you a few references which may provide you with some inspiration and insight.

In her 2025 TEDx talk on turning setbacks into success, Amy Shoenthal defines a setback as **'When you are on a path, you're moving forward and you are unexpectedly bumped backwards.'** Amy has interviewed hundreds of leaders in her career. One truth that emerged from her interviews with these leaders was that dealing with their setbacks led to their biggest successes and most successful ventures. They all came out the other side with more resilience, creativity, and strength. She explains how a setback can be seen as a green light to a new road and a new path.

Scott Galloway, in his video on how successful people deal with setbacks, says, **'The best revenge against a setback is to live your best life, a great life.'** It's really easy to get dragged down by your failures and to hold a grudge. However, successful people have an ability to reset and move on, by spending time with loved ones and engaging in hobbies and interests to clear their minds—they don't anchor themselves to despair. The important thing is, you have to keep on keeping on.

All of us will experience setbacks in our lives. We'll lose loved ones, get fired from a job, be made redundant, fail to get that promotion, experience relationships breakups, be treated unfairly at work, and experience our business failing. The key to success is our ability to mourn and move on. Most people don't recognise that every success comes with multiple failures. Yet most people have the mentality that if we fall short of perfection, we abandon hope. Experiencing a setback is not the end of the story—but imagine being at the end of the story, then looking back and telling others how you overcame that setback.

In 2008, I was working in the Middle East. With a very well-paid job travelling around the world, I was really enjoying my career. Then we had the big crash at the end of 2008, and I was made redundant. It was a quick and dirty process. From the time I was told about my redundancy to the time I left the business was only two hours…but on the upside, my wife and I enjoyed a really long lunch that afternoon.

In 2009, probably about January, I set up a new advertising, public relations, and media business. It took a few months to establish, but we got it off the ground and enjoyed serving our clients. We created a couple of products (a property magazine and a banking magazine), both of which turned over significant revenue and became very successful publications in a short time. Throughout 2009 and into 2010, our agency pitched for new business and revenues were looking good—business felt amazing. Life was good. In fact, I was feeling great.

Towards the end of 2010, we were looking at how to scale the business, scoping potential investors, and thinking, 'Okay, where can we take this next?'. Suddenly on the 17th of December, 2010, the Arab Uprising happened. There were anti-government protests, uprisings, and armed rebellions that spread across much of the Arab world, including the market where we had our office.

The next morning, I went to my office and couldn't get in. The whole building and surrounding area was barricaded with barbed wire and armed vehicles. No one could get in or out. I thought this would just be a quick 24 to 48 hour impact, but it wasn't. It went on for weeks. We simply couldn't work—our team couldn't get into the office and all our equipment was there. Unable to deliver campaigns for our clients, we lost cash fast—no one was paying us for work already completed and we couldn't earn new income which we desperately needed. Whilst our cashflow situation hurt, more importantly, the place was becoming too dangerous for my young family.

We had to leave our home and our work, while the kids had to leave their schools. We packed up and moved, leaving our home, our cars, and some of our possessions behind, with a view that we would come back to sort things out. We tried to get organised in a different part of the region, but settling into another home, with new schools, then trying to deliver for our clients from a different region in a different office, without all of our equipment or the team, was very, very challenging. In the end, it just didn't work. We tried for a whole year, but things didn't turn around. The good news was, during that year, I did return to our home, sell the house and cars, and came back to my family.

In the end, we decided to move back to the UK. As you can imagine, this experience put a lot of pressure on our family unit and ourselves, because we kept beating ourselves up saying, 'How could this have happened? Why could we have not predicted what was going to happen? We should have had a Plan B or a Plan C.' But I always lived by the mindset that you have a Plan A, and that's the *only* plan. Plan B is just a distraction.

The universe has a strange way of opening up new opportunities. As soon as we got back to the UK, I landed a senior leadership role within four weeks. We settled down, the kids got into amazing schools, and we have been here ever since. It was a real whirlwind, but a massive learning experience. It tested our mental and physical capacity, stretching our resilience, drive, and mindset. As a father and a husband, I wanted to provide for my family as the main breadwinner. It was my responsibility to make that happen and get my family settled again, and I did it, not on my own but with help from my wife, our community, our family, and a few other people. But we made it work.

I was working for a large retail company in the UK on a strategic project, feeling super-proud that I was given this project to lead and be accountable for. It was a game-changer, both for me and for the business. I established a credible team, then we developed the project strategy together and started executing the plan. Part of the process was to keep stakeholders engaged to avoid any disappointment and surprises.

Things seemed to be going really well, and I was getting very positive feedback about the way the project was evolving over time. At the end of the year when we were doing performance reviews, I went in thinking that my performance review would be very good. We went in a room, my boss walked in, and we both sat quietly for a while as she opened up with her comments that she didn't feel I had performed at the level she was expecting all year. This was news to me, as nothing was mentioned during our one-to-ones throughout the year.

One thing led to another. She did most of the talking, eventually letting me know that I wouldn't be getting my bonus and would be marked with a very low grade on my performance review for that year because of the way she felt I was managing the project. I was stunned and lost for words. I kept thinking, 'Where did this go wrong?'. I didn't see any of this coming. I'd already prepared a performance review, which showed that I'd delivered against my goals. None of that was considered. As she left the room, I reflected on the conversation (or monologue, in this instance).

Obviously, I was angry, disappointed, and stressed at that time thinking, 'How did I get this so wrong?'. But during my reflection, I started to realise that this culture was uninspiring and I didn't want to continue working for this individual. This was not because she gave me bad news, but due to how she delivered it, and her behaviour overall. So I asked myself,

'Do I really want to work in this type of organisation where they feel it's okay to land a very tough message without having any discussion about my performance through the year?'. It all felt wrong, but I can't really blame anyone else as I should have seen the signs. (Maybe I just had a blind spot.)

What I should have done is asked tougher questions through the year. I should have tested my manager and been more specific throughout the year, checking and clarifying information. I had a lot of trust in her, but what I didn't do is document some of our conversations. That was my mistake. I left the company and toxic culture soon after.

STRENGTH IN UNITY: THE IMPORTANCE OF LEANING ON OTHERS FOR SUPPORT DURING SETBACKS

When you are dealing with a setback or a failure, make sure you surround yourself with non-judgemental relationships and people. Talk to those who can help guide you, coach you, mentor you, and support your future journey. It's important to look at the problem and failure through a different lens and approach. At the end of the day, what's the worst that could happen?

If you go back to the beginning of this book, when I shared my story about my father's tragic accident, that was a real setback for the entire family, something that felt so insurmountable that it felt impossible to deal with. But they dealt with it; they became more resilient. They had the courage and became stronger together, and as a community, moved forward.

I understand why you would worry: There's a fear of consequence, especially when you're working in companies and you get something wrong. It's up to the leaders of businesses and organisations to create a psychologically safe place for people to work, where they embrace failures and setbacks, learn, and move forward. Worrying about setbacks is a simple energy drainer—it causes stress and disables you from moving forward.

Let's do a simple task. Answer these questions:

How did you react when facing a recent setback?	How did you deal with it?	What do you think you could have done better?	How will you learn from this experience?

I'm now going to share a very short exercise that I often use when I'm faced with a setback or a failure. It works for me, so I thought I'd share it. The objective is to recognise setbacks, process your emotions, and develop strategies for growth.

1. **Identify the setback.** Think of a recent situation where you faced a setback. It could be personal, academic, or professional. Now, write down a brief description of what happened.
2. **Reflect on your feelings.** Take a moment to reflect on how the setback made you feel. Write down your emotions (for example, frustration, disappointment, sadness).
3. **Analyse the situation.** Ask yourself the following questions: What were the contributing factors to this setback? Were there any warning signs that I ignored? How did I react at that moment?
4. **Identify lessons learned.** Consider what you can learn from this experience. Write down at least three key takeaways: What could I have done differently? What skills or knowledge do I need to improve? How can I prevent a similar setback in the future?
5. **Create an action plan.** Develop a plan to address each of the lessons learned. Include specific actions you can take moving forward. Set measurable goals for improvement, identifying resources or support systems that can help you.
6. **Embrace a growth mindset.** Remind yourself that setbacks are opportunities for growth. Write down a positive affirmation that reinforces this mindset.

At the end of the exercise, review your notes regularly to remind yourself of your resilience and growth.

CONCLUSION

As I conclude this chapter, I hope some of my personal stories give you the strength and resilience to move forward and tackle any setback you face. Every setback carries within it the seeds of opportunity, and by embracing a growth mindset, learning from generational differences, and adjusting our approaches, we can transform these challenges into valuable life lessons.

In a world that often emphasises success and achievement, it's crucial to remember that setbacks are not the end of the road or the end of the story, but rather stepping stones on our journey to build a new story.

YOUR 'TOUGH LOVE' MESSAGES

1. Setbacks are a natural part of life. They will invariably happen and continue to happen, and you'll continue to experience them.
2. Use setbacks to empower you to move forward in life with confidence.
3. Only you can fix your problems and setbacks, learn, adjust and grow from them. They teach us about the

foundation of how to move forward, which comes from a place within you—it's your self-belief.

Change is inevitable, so let's take a look at how you can cope with continuous change with the right self-belief.

CHAPTER 8

THE POWER OF SELF-BELIEF: BELIEVING IN YOURSELF IS THE FIRST STEP TO FULFILLING YOUR AMBITIONS

'WHEN LIFE THROWS CHALLENGES YOUR WAY, LET YOUR ACTIONS BE THE COMPASS THAT GUIDES YOU THROUGH THE STORM OF CHANGE.'

In this chapter, we'll cover how self-belief creates positive emotions when you act. Also, self-belief drives resilience, courage, and determination. We'll also walk through how you can cope with continuous change. Change is inevitable, but how we respond is a choice. Choose actions that transform uncertainty into opportunity.

When you believe in yourself, you unlock a reservoir of potential that can transform the impossible into the possible. Self-belief fuels resilience. It empowers you to rise after every fall and continue the journey towards your goals.

Often the greatest battles are fought within yourself. Self-belief is your strongest ally in this internal war. Believing in yourself is the first step to creating a life that is not just lived, but genuinely celebrated.

THE INNER BATTLE: CONFRONTING THE STRUGGLE OF SELF-DOUBT AND INSECURITY

Self-belief motivates us into action, transcending the limitations we impose. To fulfil our ambitions, we must cultivate deep-rooted faith in our capabilities.

Growing up, watching others have both parents at their sports games, I questioned why I was the only kid without a father. These constant unanswered questions, coupled with bullying and a system that punished my different thinking, decimated my self-confidence.

I struggled academically, as school rewarded memorisation over creative problem-solving. This dealt a blow to my self-belief. But my inner voice, RG, encouraged me to just do my best. However, at home, my grandfather insisted I needed to try harder and follow the rules to succeed.

INSPIRATION FROM GREAT ACHIEVERS: LESSONS IN RESILIENCE AND SUCCESS

After years of this experience, I started reading more business and motivational books, which taught me that the most valuable skills you'd need to succeed in life is not what school teaches you. The world outside of school rewards creative problem-solving. It also requires questioning everything and not following the status quo. I also realised that winners create their own opportunities.

SO WHAT'S THE FOUNDATION OF SELF-BELIEF?

The foundation of self-belief goes beyond mere feeling—it's a mindset that can be cultivated and strengthened over time. Self-belief is the unwavering conviction that we can achieve our goals, regardless of obstacles.

This foundation is vital for personal growth and reaching our full potential. Consider the stories of successful artists, entrepreneurs, and athletes who faced failures, yet persisted because they believed in themselves. Their journeys remind us that self-belief is often the first step towards achievement. It fuels motivation and fosters resilience, allowing us to rise after each fall.

To build self-belief, we must overcome doubt and fear. Recognising doubt as a natural part of the human experience is essential. Even if I wasn't academically gifted, I knew I was equally smart in my own way. Passing exams is one path, but taking action, trying new things, succeeding, failing, and making things happen in the real world is another.

CULTIVATING SELF-BELIEF: STRATEGIES TO BOOST CONFIDENCE AND EMPOWER GROWTH

In order to build more self-belief, you have to set realistic goals. Self-belief flourishes in an environment of achievable goals. When we set realistic incremental objectives, we create opportunities for success. Each small victory reinforces our self-belief, creating a positive feedback loop that encourages us to pursue larger ambitions. To set effective goals, use the SMART criteria: specific, measurable, achievable, relevant, and time-bound. I won't go into detail on this, as there are many books about SMART goals.

I thought it'd be easy just to write a book in a month. It was only over time where I set achievable goals with realistic timeframes that I had the time to actually get it done.

THE POWER OF SMALL STEPS, TAKING ACTION FOR LASTING CHANGE

Taking action is really the catalyst for growth. Action is where self-belief manifests. It is in the *doing* that we discover our potential. When we take steps towards our goals, we not only affirm our belief in ourselves, but also create tangible progress. Each action taken, whether a bold leap or a cautious step, nourishes our growth and helps us gain momentum.

Don't forget YANGA: Your Actions Nourish Growth Ambitions. Start by identifying one small action you can take today—yes, *today*—that aligns with your goals. It could be reaching out to a mentor, enrolling in a course, or dedicating time to a passion project. The key is to make that start, for inaction breeds stagnation while actions fuels growth.

Back in 2016, I signed up to do the Tough Mudder events, which consist of 25 obstacles across 12 miles. No mean feat, especially for someone who's not a good runner and probably wasn't in the best physical shape at that time. A group were going to do it and I thought I'd join them, despite only knowing a couple of members from the group of 14. The thought of getting through Tough Mudder scared me. I questioned whether I could actually get it done, or whether I would pull out somewhere near the early stages or halfway through. I watched many videos about people completing Tough Mudder, including those who didn't, which didn't help with my own self-confidence. I started hitting the gym, and it was there where I met a personal trainer whose words resonated with me.

He simply said that the only obstacle preventing me from finishing the Tough Mudder course was in my own mind. If I think I'm not capable of doing it, I won't be. But if I can visualise the future goal of walking or running across the finish line, I'd be able to do it; it's all down to me.

Ready for Tough Mudder a few months later, we set off. Getting over those 14-foot walls, climbing up ropes, diving into ice-cold muddy water even though I couldn't really swim? Digging myself out of a small smoke-filled hole in the ground? Feeling a little bit claustrophobic while running through water and over hay bales, getting zapped by car batteries right the way through to cross the finish line? I completed it in four-and-a-half hours. I was tired, muddy, wet, cut in various places, and bruised all over. But I loved the experience, and earned my cold beer. (I even have a T-shirt to prove I finished it!)

I experienced an immense sense of joy, satisfaction, and achievement from Tough Mudder, but I'm not going to do that again. I got through it because I had a really good support structure, people with positive influences on me who encouraged me to train and give it a go. This wasn't the case at the beginning when I signed up, where I was surrounded by people who said, 'Ugh, that's not something you can do. You're not so great. You don't feel very strong. You don't look very strong. Are you really going to do it? You'll probably pull out.' But I blocked the negative talk and created more positive self-talk.

THE COMPANY WE KEEP: SURROUNDING OURSELVES WITH UPLIFTING INFLUENCES

To nurture self-belief, we have to seek out individuals who uplift and inspire us—friends, family, mentors, even online communities. Share your ambitions and aspirations with them and allow their encouragement to reinforce your self-belief.

Moreover, consider eliminating or distancing yourself from negative influences that undermine your confidence. This could mean reducing time spent with critical individuals or curating your social media feeds to focus on positivity and inspiration.

The road to self-belief is not always smooth. It requires patience, persistence, and a willingness to embrace vulnerability. Yet as we cultivate this belief within ourselves, we unlock the door to growth and the fulfilment of our ambitions. In this journey, remember that self-belief ebbs and flows influenced by our experiences and the world around us.

DAILY ACTIONS, THE KEY TO CONTINUOUS PROGRESS

This book is very much about you taking action. Taking action often serves as a powerful catalyst for positive emotions, creating a ripple effect that enhances our overall wellbeing. When we step outside of our comfort zones and engage in activities that align with our goals or passions, we ignite a sense of accomplishment and empowerment. The simple act of moving forward, whether it's tackling a new project, pursuing a hobby, or making a difficult decision, can flood our minds and bodies with feelings of joy, excitement, and satisfaction.

Moreover, the act of taking action can help to alleviate feelings of anxiety and uncertainty. This was definitely the case when I actually signed up for Tough Mudder and went through that entire process. Negative emotions can often fester when we find ourselves in a state of inaction or indecision, leading to a cycle of self-doubt and fear. However, when we choose to act, even in small ways, we disrupt this cycle. Each step forward brings clarity and a sense of control.

Additionally, taking action often opens doors to new experiences and connections, further enriching our emotional landscape. Engaging with others, whether through collaboration, volunteering, or simply sharing our journey, can foster a sense of belonging and community. These social interactions can amplify our positive emotions.

As we take action, we not only cultivate our own growth, but also inspire and uplift those around us, creating a shared atmosphere of positivity and encouragement. In this way, the act of taking action becomes not just a personal achievement, but a collective celebration.

Clara was known for her unwavering spirit and zest for life. But her world shifted beneath her— from job changes to family dynamics, she navigated continuous upheaval.

Yet instead of succumbing to the chaos, Clara leaned into her self-belief—a quiet force nurtured through experience. When her company downsized, the familiar pang of uncertainty arose. But this time she paused, reminding herself of the obstacles she'd overcome. Her self-belief became a beacon, illuminating the path ahead.

Rather than fearing change, she chose to embrace it as an opportunity. Drawing on her resilience, she explored new possibilities—enrolling in courses, connecting with others, and starting a passion-fuelled side business.

Clara discovered that her self-belief wasn't just a shield, but a wellspring of strength empowering her to confront challenges head-on. As she navigated the waves of change, Clara became a source of inspiration for those around her.

CONQUERING DOUBTS AND FEARS, BREAKING FREE FROM THEIR CONTROL

Doubts and fear dominate our lives. Usually, these come from external influences. Many people will quickly pass judgement, and then our internal voice starts questioning our ability and worth.

My self-belief was knocked down and I built it back up. Before 1997, I was always told I needed people around me, my family, my friends. I wasn't good on my own. I wouldn't cope on my own. In early 1997, I secured a job in the Middle East. (In Saudi Arabia, in fact.) It was a big move. I had a well-paid, credible career with a bank in the UK, so why would I want to go to Saudi Arabia? It was an amazing opportunity to work with another bank out there among incredible people with a strong human connection, to help them establish a new marketing communication department.

I had the travel bug. Wanting to go and explore the world, I signed a contract and accepted the position despite everybody around me trying to influence my decision, telling me I wouldn't be able to cope, it's not the right thing to do, and I should stay close to my family and friends and be more supportive. I decided: 'I'm going.' Of course, it would be difficult to leave everyone behind. I'd never done that before.

In February 1997, I departed for Riyadh, Saudi Arabia, soon settling down into an expat community and started my work. Was it hard living on my own? Absolutely. Was it hard fending for myself? Absolutely, it was. Did I enjoy the experience? A hundred percent. I created a new community of people who supported my career, who encouraged me to keep moving forward. Adjusting to the new culture was very difficult, but I loved learning about it. I really enjoyed meeting local people, having conversations, sharing a shisha pipe, and eventually getting into coffee. (I actually didn't drink coffee until I went to Saudi Arabia at age 27.)

At the end of the two-year cycle, my contract was up. We'd had a very successful two years, launching many new products and a new brand while improving our market share. My leaving party from the bank said it all. I had so many people there wishing me luck and all the best for the future. I was overwhelmed. I just didn't expect so many people to come.

Another example of where my self-belief was impacted was when I was Marketing Director of a financial service brand covering 18 countries across the Middle East and North Africa. I had led a team to prepare a very detailed plan, in preparation to launch a product across nine markets simultaneously—the first time the product would be launched across that many markets all at once. I knew it would be highly complex, but we had the right team, the right resources, and the right attitude to make it work.

I was in a board meeting presenting the final plan when a couple of the board members looked up, disagreed with the plan, and pretty much said: 'It cannot be done. You won't be able to do it.' Their comments shook me, as expected. They're board members, I thought. They're more experienced. Yet while they've been around a lot longer, my mindset and state of readiness meant that I wasn't going to take no for an answer. What I was looking for was a more supportive environment—and I knew if I didn't get that 'Yes', the entire project would be stopped. If that happened, all the time invested by many, many people, coupled with significant resources worldwide, would be wasted.

At that moment, I realised that the only person who was going to stop me from moving forward was me. I took a deep breath, got my self-confidence back, believed in the project and the people behind it, and answered all the questions and challenges that the board put forward. Nine months later, we launched the product across nine markets simultaneously, and it turned out to be one of the most successful launches ever carried out in that business.

Through a clear sense of self-belief, I took full accountability, set realistic goals, and took action. When you take action, you get a dopamine hit.

Now, try this exercise:

Write down a time when your self-belief had hit rock bottom. (If it hasn't hit rock bottom, just remember a time when it was low.)

What was the situation?	What made you feel that your self-belief was impacted?	What did you do to overcome that?	What could you have done differently to avoid feeling that your self-belief was so low?

As we reach the conclusion, my parting 'tough love' message to you is the following:

- You cannot wait decades to believe in yourself.
- You shouldn't feel afraid to use your voice and ask for what you want, whether that's at home or at work. Question those who say no. Be bold.
- Have the courage to carry out your plan, without being afraid to express your opinion. Keep your mind open and your spirits high, without feeling the need to apologise for any of it.

CONCLUSION

Creating greater self-belief is a state of mind, which you can keep developing and strengthening over time. Roll the dice and take action, as this will serve as a powerful catalyst for positive emotions.

Now, write down three positive affirmations. For example,

- If you doubt your abilities at work, your affirmations could be: 'I'm capable and skilled at my job. I bring unique value to my team. I overcome challenges with confidence.'
- Then think about daily practice. For the next week, take a few minutes each day to read your affirmations aloud. Stand in front of a mirror if possible, saying each of them with conviction.
- Visualise yourself embodying these statements.

When you experience turbulent times, your self-belief plays a vital role—as does your ability to refrain from overthinking.

CHAPTER 9

THE PARALYSING GRIP OF OVERTHINKING: MIND TRAPS MUST BE REFRAMED AND SIMPLIFIED

'THE MORE YOU THINK, THE LESS YOU UNDERSTAND.'

—HABIB SADEGHI

We have all been there. We have all overthought an issue, a problem, a challenge, even an opportunity. Our minds are just wired that way. Our minds are like water—when it's turbulent, it's difficult to see; when it's calm, everything becomes clear. Ask yourself the question: What's the worst that can happen? Is it a matter of life or death? In some instances, it probably is, but even then, these are setbacks that we all have to face at some point in our lives. At these moments, having clarity of thought is what will get us through the other side.

Let me share with you some common causes of overthinking.

- **Fear of Failure:** Many of us have concerns about making mistakes or not meeting expectations, which then lead to excessive rumination on decisions and actions.
- **Delivering flawless results:** This sometimes causes individuals to obsess over details, making it difficult to move forward. This is when you strive for perfectionism.
- **Facing up to uncertainty:** Ambiguity often impacts our roles, responsibilities, or project outcomes and creates anxiety, prompting over-analysis of situations.

We often face situations when the consequences of decisions are significant. Individuals may overthink to ensure that they make the right choice. This is when the stakes are really high, and quite often we look at previous negative experiences or criticisms that we faced, making us more cautious and prone to overthinking future actions.

THE OVERTHINKER'S MIND, A TANGLE OF THOUGHTS AND EMOTIONS

When I was much younger, I was an obsessive overthinker. Yet those who know me now probably find that statement surprising. It's true, though—I used to overthink everything.

What I remember most is when I would become overly fearful of something tragic happening to the rest of my family, exactly like it did for my father. I used to wonder: What would I do? Where would I stay? Who would look after me if something happened to them? This went on for years, because I just could not remove it from my mind. I didn't know how.

I also overthought what the teachers would say, especially as I wasn't very academically bright and my grades were always very low. I knew I would face up to consequences and overthink their response to my poor homework or lack of attention.

When I was bullied at school, I'd dwell on the possibility of the bullies coming after me and causing trouble at my home, then overthink about how I would handle that.

I would also overthink about whether I could actually make my family proud of me. Could I please them with my results, outcomes, and achievements? Could I deliver on my father's and grandfather's dream of being better-educated, getting a university degree and securing a lucrative job, and eventually settling down?

UNDERSTANDING OVERTHINKING: THE MENTAL MAZE OF EXCESSIVE ANALYSIS

The incessant chatter of overthinking involves a relentless loop of analysis, doubt, and fear that can transform even the simplest decisions into monumental challenges. As we navigate our daily lives, the weight of overthinking can lead us into a toxic frame of mind, obscuring clarity and complicating our paths.

Overthinking is more than just a fleeting thought or moment of hesitation—it's a cognitive pattern that can rapidly spiral into anxiety and self-doubt. What starts as a simple question or decision quickly morphs into an overwhelming dissection of every possibility, outcome, and potential failure.

Consider deciding what to eat for dinner, a straightforward choice which can turn into an exhausting ordeal. Should I eat healthily? What if my family dislikes the food? Is it too expensive? Have I accommodated everyone's dietary needs? The process of overthinking transforms a mundane decision into a persistent source of stress, draining our energy and mental resources.

Overthinking creates a labyrinth of worry, making us feel trapped. Instead of approaching challenges with a clear mind, we get lost in a deep dive of analysis. This cognitive pattern, though perhaps well-intentioned, ends up hindering our progress and sacrificing our peace of mind.

Do you remember a time you took quick action towards completing a task which failed, resulting in you thinking about the results for a long time afterwards? Overthinking creates a toxic frame of mind, with its toxicity lying in its ability to distort reality. When we overanalyse, we often magnify the negative while minimising or dismissing the positive. Our minds become breeding grounds for worst-case scenarios, undermining our confidence in the process.

In relationships, overthinking can create misunderstandings and tension. A simple comment might be dissected, leading to one person questioning the other's intentions and harbouring self-doubt, a process which erodes the connections we cherish.

When younger, I would avoid situations altogether as a way to deal with challenges, in the hopes that the problems would just go away. But they don't. They may be parked in the back of the mind, but eventually they catch up with you; these scenarios play out even worse years later.

BREAKING FREE FROM OVERTHINKING: STRATEGIES FOR EMPOWERED DECISION-MAKING

To combat the toxic effects of overthinking, we must adopt a new approach, one that emphasises simplicity and clarity. Rethinking our mindset involves recognising that not every challenge requires exhaustive analysis. Instead, we can embrace a more intuitive approach, allowing ourselves to make decisions based on what feels right rather than what we fear.

Let me share five strategies to simplify your thought process and reclaim your mental space.

1. **Set time limits.** Give yourself a specific timeframe to make a decision. When the time is up, commit to your choice without further rumination. This can help break the cycle of overthinking.
2. **Prioritise action over perfection.** Accept that not every decision will be perfect. Focus on taking action, even if it's small. Remember, taking action creates progress and forward movement. The momentum gained from making a choice can help alleviate the grip of overthinking.
3. **Limit information intake.** In our information-saturated world, it is easy to fall into a trap of seeking more data and drowning yourself in more information before making a decision. Instead, focus on gathering *only* the essential information needed to move forward.
4. **Challenge negative thoughts.** When you catch yourself spiralling into overthinking, challenge those thoughts. Ask yourself if they're based on facts or assumptions. Often, you'll find that your fears are unfounded.
5. **Seek support.** Don't hesitate to reach out to friends, family, or colleagues for a different perspective. Sometimes, an outside viewpoint can shed light on what we may be missing or help us see the simplicity in the situation.

These techniques help simplify our path forward. Remember, simplicity is not synonymous with ignorance—rather, it's about clarity and intention. When we approach challenges with a mindset focused on simplicity, we can navigate our lives with greater ease. By cutting through the noise of overthinking, we create space for creativity, spontaneity, and joy. Embracing a simplified approach to life allows us to focus on what truly matters.

As we free ourselves from the paralysing grip of overthinking, we open ourselves up to new possibilities and experiences. The journey towards overcoming overthinking is not just about silencing the inner critic; it also involves cultivating a mindset that values clarity and action. By rethinking our approach to daily challenges and simplifying our paths, we can transform the way we engage with the world, fostering a healthier, more fulfilling existence.

Overthinking at work can manifest in various situations where pressure and stresses are high.

I used to spend excessive time analysing every possible outcome of a decision, fearing the repercussions of making a mistake—wanting to be perfect, I didn't accept the necessity of making mistakes. This led to analysis paralysis, and I struggled to choose a course of action on many occasion.

I remember one time when a project was going over budget and I had to make a decision on whether to spend £10,000 more on the projects. At that time, this was a lot of money, and we had already invested £100,000. I obsessively pored over all the information, repeatedly looking at different data to understand what the impact of that extra £10,000 would be. I couldn't even sleep at night thinking about making a decision to spend another £10,000 on top of the £100,000 we had already spent. I became obsessed with the potential consequences if something went wrong, rather than the fact that given we'd already invested the £100,000, another £10,000 would get the projects over the line and allow us to reap the rewards of delivering the project. Eventually, I decided that we should invest the extra £10,000. The project was successful and the company reaped the rewards—so no harm done, apart from my mental health throughout the process.

Those who know me understand that I am a confident presenter both on stage and off. Earlier in my career, though, I would obsess over every detail, including the slides, the timing of each one, and even how they would be perceived by the audience. The resultant anxiety distracted me from the actual content and delivery.

When I was in my late teens and just starting university, I joined a multi-level marketing organisation selling perfumes and jewellery. Over time, I built a very strong network organisation, receiving cheques in the post for the products sold by my organisation. That was a great outcome, and my business started being successful.

One day, my organisational leader asked me to present at the annual conference. While this was a major opportunity to communicate my message in front of the whole organisation, it was also very scary. I started feeling anxious and stressed. When I asked him how many people there would be in the room and he said 400, my head went into a spin. I hadn't even presented to a group of *50* people back then, so how was I going to keep the audience's attention with *400* people in the room?

My overthinking went into overdrive. In the end, it was my organisation leader who actually put more calmness into the process. He said to me: 'Look. You know the detail, you know how you've built the organization, all you have to do is share your story. Keep it simple—you know how to do it and win.' He also reassured me that even the best presenters feel nervous when they get on stage. All they do is control their nerves, which only comes through preparation, preparation, and more preparation. His vote of confidence in my abilities enabled me to create more self-confidence, deliver a brilliant presentation, and receive rave reviews. I did it. Everything else after that felt a breeze.

THE WEIGHT OF OTHERS' OPINIONS: HOW EXTERNAL VOICES FUEL OVERTHINKING

Constantly considering others can exacerbate overthinking, anxiety, and stress. This diverts focus from your own needs and desires, leading to unhappiness. Consistently prioritising others' thoughts, feelings, and expectations above your own wellbeing is detrimental.

This habitual self-sacrifice creates an internal conflict, leaving you torn between fulfilling responsibilities to others and honouring your own aspirations. Remember, your wellbeing must come first.

Moreover, this preoccupation with others' opinions and feelings can foster anxiety. You may find yourself overanalysing interactions, worrying about how your actions will be perceived, or feeling guilty for prioritising your own needs. This cycle of worry can become exhausting, leaving little room for joy or self-acceptance. When we allow ourselves to be consumed by the thoughts of others, we often lose sight of our own identity.

Additionally, the constant comparison to others can exacerbate feelings of inadequacy. When you focus too much on how others are doing, you may overlook your own progress and achievements. It's exactly what I did during my performance review in my early 30s, leading to a distorted view of my own self-worth.

Practising self-care during stressful times is often essential for maintaining mental and physical wellbeing. Here are five examples of how to engage in self-care:

- **Prioritise sleep.** Ensure you get enough restful sleep each night, establishing a calming bedtime routine and aiming for consistent sleep and wake times.
- **Stay connected.** Reach out to friends, family, colleagues, or support groups. Talking about your feelings and experiences can provide comfort and perspective.
- **Limit news consumption.** I've done this recently and my brain feels so much clearer. While staying informed is important, excessive exposure to stressful news can

increase anxiety. Set boundaries on how much news you consume each day. Don't forget, news is a 'moment in time' piece of information and sometimes it's exaggerated.
- **Set boundaries.** Learn to say no when necessary. Protect your time and energy by setting boundaries with work and personal commitments.
- **Practise gratitude.** Take time each day to reflect on things you are grateful for. Keeping a gratitude journal, if that works for you, can help shift focus away from stressors and highlight the positive aspects of life.
- Incorporating these self-care practices into your routine can help you manage stress more effectively and promote overall wellbeing.

DECLUTTERING THE MIND: ACHIEVING CLARITY THROUGH MENTAL ORGANISATION

It's really important to declutter your mind and achieve clarity of thought, like you would declutter your wardrobe every now and again and send some of the old clothes to charity or sell them through an online platform. Your mind always needs a refresh, so take action today to start accepting the situation and decluttering.

Let me now share a couple of stories that will bring the idea of overthinking to life. (While these are real-life stories, obviously the names I'm using are not real.)

Emily, a marketing manager known for her creativity and drive, faced a high-stakes project deadline. Suddenly, she experienced an unexpected bout of anxiety. I noticed her overthinking every aspect—the messaging, visuals, budget, even font choices. As her mind raced with worst-case scenarios, she worked through the night.

The next day, Emily arrived exhausted and stressed. During the team meeting, she opened up about her fears. Her colleagues listened empathetically, sharing their own experiences. Encouraged by their understanding, Emily realised she wasn't alone.

Refocusing her energy, Emily set aside perfection and outlined a simple plan. Collaborating with her team, she found joy in the creative process again. Channelling their renewed determination into action, they worked late nights fuelled by passion.

When launch day arrived, the campaign was met with enthusiasm. Reflecting on her journey, Emily realised embracing vulnerability and teamwork had transformed her approach. The stress that once clouded her mind became a stepping stone towards growth and success. Emily felt grateful for an experience that taught her the power of resilience.

My next story is about Mark, who had always prided himself on being the main breadwinner for his family. He was a senior lawyer at a reputable firm and worked tirelessly to climb the corporate ladder, providing a comfortable life for his wife and two children. But everything changed one afternoon when he received the news that due to company restructuring, he was being made redundant. I was coaching Mark during this time, and it was a very difficult period for him. Mark explained that the moment he hung up the phone, a wave of panic washed over him. Questions flooded his mind. How would his wife react? What would she feel? Would she feel disappointed? Would they have to sell their home? Will they be homeless? Where would they stay? He had always been the provider, and the thought of losing the role filled him with dread.

As he drove home, the weight of his thoughts grew heavier. He envisioned his wife's face when he broke the news. Imagining her worry and concern, what would he say? How could he reassure her and the family that everything would be okay? The more he overthought it, the more anxious he became. Each scenario in his mind painted a picture of despair and uncertainty. When he got home, he finally plucked up the courage to have a talk with his wife. She noticed his unease and anxiety as they sat down to talk. With a deep breath, Mark shared the news of his redundancy. As the words left his mouth, he watched his wife's expression shift from surprise to concern.

During our coaching sessions, his doubts still lingered. He spent a number of days in a haze, searching for jobs while constantly replaying the conversation with his wife in his mind. Each time, he felt the fear creeping back. He was reminded of his encouraging words from his wife, but he still felt the struggle. One day, a couple of weeks after his redundancy, he began networking with former colleagues and people he knew from outside of the industry. He started exploring freelance opportunities and considered starting his own legal consultancy. With the right support from his colleagues, his ex-colleagues, his network, his family, and me as his coach, he began to regain confidence.

Mark was actually surprised by the number of connections willing to help, and soon secured a few projects that allowed him to contribute financially while also spending time with his family. Mark soon realised that while losing his job had initially sparked fear and overthinking, it had also opened up new opportunities. Navigating the challenges, he learned that being the breadwinner didn't just mean bringing home the paycheque. It also meant being present and resilient for his family.

As both these stories demonstrate, you can overcome overthinking by sharing your concerns, talking about what's on your mind, and creating a robust support structure—a network of people who can help you.

A FEW SIMPLE TECHNIQUES TO GET YOU STARTED

Let me now share a simple technique I use to overcome any overthinking which I experience.

Set a thinking time. Allocate a specific time, it could be 15 minutes, it could be 20 minutes, each day to think about your concerns. Outside of this time, remind yourself that you can address these thoughts later. I usually do this at 8:00 in the morning and I spend 30 minutes every single morning thinking about some of the challenges and issues I need to overcome and address.

CONCLUSION

Life's complexities stem from the daily choices and responsibilities we face. With abundant information and expectations, it's easy to become overwhelmed. This can lead to analysis paralysis—the fear of making the wrong choice, or the pressure to achieve perfection, stifles our ability to act. Overthinking, second-guessing, and hesitation set in.

To combat this paralysis, we must embrace simplicity. Facing life's complexities head on requires a shift in mindset—away from the trappings of perfection and towards a focus on progress. By simplifying our approach, we liberate ourselves to take action, learn, and grow.

Simplifying our approach to decision-making can help us cut through the noise and focus on what truly matters. By prioritising our core values and setting clear goals, we can create a framework that guides our choices without unnecessary complications. Simplifying doesn't mean ignoring important details. Instead, it actually means homing in on the essentials that align with our personal vision and overall wellbeing.

Keeping things simple fosters clarity and enhances our ability to respond to challenges with confidence. When we reduce the clutter in our minds, we free ourselves to act decisively and purposefully.

I will end with some 'tough love' messages for you.

- **Don't listen to the naysayers and dream-killers.** If you listened to everyone, you wouldn't get anywhere. (Maybe that's where you are right now.)
- **Everything can be simple.** You are the one that makes your life complicated, so silence that negative inner voice.
- **Things will go wrong in life.** It's how you think about it that matters, giving you the ability to take action. It is never too late to start something new.
- **When we reduce clutter in our minds, we free ourselves** to act decisively and purposefully.

This helps us to be in the positive frame of mind. How do we do that? Let's find out in the next chapter.

CHAPTER 10
FROM WORRIER TO ACCEPTOR: EMBRACING LIFE'S UNCERTAINTIES AND CONSERVING ENERGY

'ACCEPTANCE IS THE FIRST STEP TO CHANGE LIFE. IT'S 10% WHAT HAPPENS TO US, 90% HOW WE REACT TO IT.'

Things will go wrong along the way, yet you should enjoy the journey anyway. After all, it's your story. For many, this internal storm manifests as worry, a constant cycle of 'what ifs' and 'if onlys' that drain our energy and cloud our minds. But what if we could transform that worry into acceptance? What if we could learn to let go of the burdens that weigh us down and embrace life as it comes? This chapter will explore the journey from being a worrier to becoming an acceptor, focusing on how to eliminate the drivers of wasted energy that hinder our peace of mind at this point. Now, let me take you back to the beginning of this book.

NO TIME TO WORRY: EMBRACING ACTION OVER ANXIETY

Imagine the worry my family had back in March 1970. My grandfather, who lost his eldest son; my grandmother, who lost her son; my mother, who lost her husband and was widowed at the age of 22—they must have all gone through immense worry when my father passed away in a tragic car accident, overthinking and worrying about their futures and what would happen. How would they live? How would they cope? Who would help them? Where do they go? They must have been thinking: If only he didn't go to his cricket match, if only he had stayed at home, things would have been different. Maybe if he *did* stay at home that day or that weekend, he would have still been here today.

Now, back to the present. With everything moving at a rapid pace, the pressure of work is increasing, as is the pressure at home. We seem to be worrying about our kids, our lives, our homes, our safety, and our jobs. So, let's dissect and understand worry.

So, what *is* worry? Worry is a natural human response, a mechanism developed to protect us from potential threats. However, it often spirals out of control, leading us to dwell on things we cannot change. To break free from this cycle, we must first acknowledge the sources of our worry. Are they rooted in me—in fear or failure, the desire for control, or perhaps the need for approval from others? By identifying these energy consumers, we can begin to dismantle their power over us. Let's now talk about the energy drain of worry. Wasted energy is often tied to our worries. Every minute spent ruminating over past mistakes or fretting about future uncertainties is a minute lost in the present. This energy drain not only affects our mental health, but also impacts our physical wellbeing.

We can't change the past—it's already happened, so there's no point worrying about it. We also can't predict the future—we don't know what will happen, so there's no point trying. Given these facts, why waste energy fretting over the unknown?

The solution is to live in the present moment and stop worrying. Around 90% of the things we stress about will never actually occur. Yet people spend countless hours, days, and months consumed by these imagined scenarios.

Therefore, we need to shift from a 'worrier' mentality to one of acceptance. This fundamental perspective change is key.

LETTING GO OF WORRY: EMBRACING ACCEPTANCE IN UNCERTAIN TIMES

Journaling can help us acknowledge our worries while also reminding us of the beauty and potential of the present moment. We need to master the art of letting go. Letting go is an essential part of acceptance, involving releasing the need to control outcomes and embracing uncertainty.

One effective technique is to create a worry list. Write down your worries, then categorise them into two groups: things you can control and things you cannot.

My worries	What I can control	What I cannot control

For the things you cannot control, start by visualising each worry as a balloon released into the sky. This simple act can provide a profound sense of relief and freedom. Go ahead, try it!

To transition from 'worrier' to 'acceptor', you must create a positive energy environment. So, surround yourself with uplifting influences and supportive friends. Decluttering your space can boost mental clarity, allowing you to focus on what truly matters. Setting boundaries is a crucial step to eliminate wasted energy—many of us expend effort trying to please others or take on responsibilities that don't serve our wellbeing. By establishing clear boundaries, we protect our time and energy.

Social media often fuels worry. The constant consumption of content blurs our sense of what's good, bad, or ugly, leading to unnecessary stress. If your life feels dull, perhaps your phone addiction is the problem. To overcome worry and thrive, then, you must remove the things holding you back. Disable notifications, stop defaulting to your phone, and make room for new, enriching experiences.

WORRY IS A CHOICE, SO EMPOWER YOURSELF TO SHIFT PERSPECTIVE

Brian Keane, in his book *Rewire Your Mindset*, says, 'Don't let the biggest enemy sit between your ears.' What he's alluding to there is that you are in control of your worry. If you worry, that's down to you. You also have a choice not to get overwhelmed with issues and challenges, but to face them head on instead by taking action and getting on with it. We all live in a fast-paced, forever-changing world. Change is becoming the norm—in fact, it's no longer change, it's just part of everyday life. Consequently, we should create a new word for change.

When we face the change that's often the instigator towards our worries, *we* determine whether we accept or worry about the situation. So, embracing change becomes really important. Acceptance is also about embracing change, especially as life is inherently unpredictable, and our ability to adapt is crucial to our mental wellbeing. Instead of fearing change, we can view it as an opportunity for growth. Each new experience, whether positive or negative, can teach us valuable lessons and bring us closer to our authentic selves.

Every challenge becomes a stepping stone, guiding you toward a more positive and empowering narrative. As you shift your thinking, cultivate curiosity and openness. Don't view setbacks as failures, but instead as vital experiences enriching your story. Each twist and turn provides insights that contribute to your evolving journey. By savouring these moments, you'll appreciate life's richness—every thread, bright or dark, adds depth.

Creating a new story involves consciously choosing the thoughts and beliefs that define you.

We often strive for perfection, but embracing imperfection can strengthen us. Life is filled with both triumphs and trials as we navigate our unique journeys. Missed opportunities, failed relationships, unexpected setbacks—these moments can feel overwhelming. However, accepting these realities is a crucial step towards personal growth and resilience.

Embracing this truth allows us to transform challenges into stepping stones, not stumbling blocks.

When we face adversity, it's easy to succumb to feelings of defeat or despair, yet it's essential to recognise that these experiences are not the end of our journey, but rather an integral part of it. Each misstep teaches us valuable lessons, instilling strength and resilience that we might not have discovered otherwise, like a muscle that grows stronger through resistance. Characters are forged through hardship, in the process of accepting that mistakes and setbacks are part of life.

In 1994, my family had been planning a major event. This process had been ongoing for months, but it felt like years, with everything down to the wire. We had every detail planned out precisely, except for one. In the late hours of 26th August, my grandfather and mentor GR suddenly passed away from a brain aneurysm. It all happened very quickly; within about 10 minutes, he died in my arms.

My immediate reaction was obviously shock, surprise, disbelief. This was totally unexpected, but as the information started settling down in my brain, I started worrying: What's going to happen tomorrow, when we have hundreds of guests arriving for our event? What do I do now? Whom do I ask for guidance? GR was my guide, my leader at home; he took responsibility, and would know what to do. I then started worrying about what would happen to my grandmother, whom I lived with at the time. How would she cope? I worried about the funeral and how to arrange it. (At just 25 years old, I hadn't managed one before.)

Life just didn't feel fair. My resilience and courage had to come through. I needed to reframe my mindset, rather than be imprisoned by it. I had to break free and think about what lay ahead and how I could take better control of it. I couldn't control that situation that happened, but what I *could* control is how I responded to it. With determination, I could take more responsibility and make things work for my family and everyone around me. By doing this, I could show them I was capable of taking control. This challenge became a true life lesson. I had to accept that things would go wrong, cultivating a mindset that embraced resilience. So instead of fearing the failure and worrying about what would happen, I had to learn to view the situation as a necessary part of my journey.

The shift in my perspective fostered a sense of empowerment, allowing me to approach life's decisions with courage and confidence. We learn to navigate life's uncertainties with grace, understanding that setbacks do not define us but rather mould us into more capable and compassionate individuals.

LET'S DO THE 'WORRIER TO ACCEPTOR' EXERCISE

Here's a simple exercise to transform your worries into opportunities for growth and action.

- **Write down your worry.** Take a few minutes to write down a specific worry that has been troubling you. Be as clear and detailed as possible about what you are worried about.
- **Analyse the worry.** Reflect on the following questions: What is the root of this worry? How does it affect your daily life? What is the worst-case scenario, and how likely is it to happen?
- **Reframe the worry.** Shift your perspective by asking: What can I learn from this worry? Are there any hidden opportunities in this situation? How can this worry motivate me to take decisive action or change something for the better?
- **Identify actionable steps based on your reflections.** List one or two actionable steps you can take to address the worry of all the opportunities presented. For example, if you're worried about a job interview, you might prepare by practising common interview questions. If you're concerned about a relationship, consider having an open conversation with the person involved.
- **Create a positive affirmation.** Write a positive affirmation that counters your worry. For instance: 'I am capable of handling challenges and turning them into opportunities.' Or: 'Every worry offers a chance to grow and learn.'
- **Reflect and practise gratitude.** Spend a few moments reflecting on your journey from worrier to acceptor, writing down three things you are grateful for in your life right now. This will help shift your mindset to a more positive state.

Repeat this exercise whenever you feel overwhelmed by worry. Over time, you'll develop a habit of viewing challenges as opportunities for growth and resilience.

NAVIGATING EMOTIONS, BALANCING HEART AND MIND DURING DIFFICULT DECISIONS

Another story took place when I was Head of Marketing of a big global financial service brand. We were running many events, and in this particular instance I had poured my heart and soul into a major customer event, only to receive lukewarm reviews and feedback from my leadership and other stakeholders. My team and I had worked exceptionally hard day and night to get all the detail right, dot the i's, cross the t's, and make this event one of the best we could…yet something was missing. My stakeholders just did not have the same enthusiasm as I had.

Instead of waiting until afterwards to give me feedback, they shared it at the event, when spirits were high and we had customers to manage. This obviously crushed me, and I reflected for days as to why they felt compelled to share feedback at the event instead of afterwards. I still don't understand why certain leaders like to do that; maybe it's related to being in a position of power and control, who knows. The point is, some people don't really think about their impact on others. I soon found solace in the realisation that the experience was not a reflection of my worth, but rather an opportunity for growth.

I used the feedback to improve how I could deliver the next event and the process building up to it. In doing so, I experimented with different processes to make sure the stakeholders were engaged and had their say along the journey. It goes without saying that the next event received rave reviews, and it became clear that the earlier setback had been a vital part of my professional journey.

In my professional career, I've been let go three times; I've also had to let go of many people, including team members and even non-team members. (To be honest, I've lost count of exactly how many.) When I first had to let go of a team member, I worried about the impact on them and their families. What will they do? How will they cope? I also worried about how they would perceive me going forward, because perception was very important to me. But entering a conversation where you're about to let go of a team member, and you're going in with a mindset of worry, is not a good thing. To avoid this, you have to compartmentalise—that is, separate the conversation at hand from your emotional state. When emotions get in the way, the negotiations become harder. They become blurry.

The organisation didn't win at that time, because I gave away more than they expected (in terms of what the other employee could benefit from). It wasn't a balanced exchange, as I wasn't in the right frame of mind. But over time, my resilience, courage, and confidence came through. I learned how to deal with the conversation at hand versus my emotions, which stood me in good stead as I scaled the corporate ladder.

Letting go of an individual (or an entire team) is never easy—but it's part and parcel of strong leadership, and it's becoming more frequent in recent years. My advice to anyone in a corporate job is this: Don't worry about losing your job, because new opportunities are always out there. However, stay two steps ahead of your organisation, so you can choose to exit under your terms. Jobs for life don't exist any longer, so set your own standards.

I was talking to a friend recently who had just lost his senior marketing role in a big grocery retailer. While talking to me over a coffee, he shared all of his worries. We paused when the conversation got quite emotional, giving him time to reset and reframe. When he asked for my advice on what to do, my words to him were: 'If you keep looking for the worst, you will miss all the opportunities for growth.' He had to change the lens through which he saw the world, so that he could really view challenges as possibilities. Instead, he was constantly dwelling on the negatives, which paralyse you rather than protecting you.

In short, he had to learn to focus on solutions instead of problems. My final comments to him (a bit of a 'tough love' message) were:

- Stop being a spectator in your own life by fixating on what's wrong.
- Take action and create the change you want to see.

He thanked me for the conversation the next day, appreciating my directness. He said that he actually woke up with a different frame of mind, and wanted to keep talking about where he's going next.

Embracing imperfection fosters deeper connections. When we share our struggles, we create space for authenticity and empathy. We realise we're not alone—everyone faces their own battles. By accepting that things will go wrong, we cultivate a community of support and understanding. Resilience is a shared journey. Moving forward, carry the knowledge that it's okay when things don't go as planned—with jobs, relationships, or opinions. Embrace the imperfections, learn from the challenges, and trust each experience contributes to your personal growth.

CONCLUSION

Every misstep adds depth and richness to your story. With each obstacle overcome, you emerge stronger, more resilient, and ready to face whatever comes next. In this acceptance lies the true essence of the human experience—the ability to rise, adapt and thrive, no matter what life throws our way.

You control your response and how you react to situations, and it's up to you to take responsibility for your own reactions. Moving from being a worrier to an acceptor requires patience, self-compassion, and a willingness to confront your fears. As we learn to release wasted energy drivers and embrace acceptance, we open ourselves up to a life of greater peace, joy, and fulfilment. Remember, acceptance is not a destination, but a continuous process.

So when moving from worrier to acceptor, let me leave you with these three 'tough love' messages.

- Your perspective is your choice—you don't need permission.
- If you geniunely want to change your reality, change your perspective.
- You can't control every situation, so let it go.

Words often lead to our worries (what someone said, how they said it, what you said, and how you said it). As it is often our conversations that shape the way we feel, let's explore this in the next chapter.

CHAPTER 11

NAVIGATING CONVERSATIONS FROM INNER THOUGHTS TO OUTER VOICES: CONVERSATIONS THAT SHAPE US

'WORDS ARE THE MOST POWERFUL DRUG USED BY MANKIND.'

—RUDYARD KIPLING

Communication works best for those who work at it, and is often considered one of the most important skills in today's fast-paced world. Effective communication facilitates collaboration, enhances relationships, and ensures that information is shared clearly and efficiently in a diverse and interconnected environment.

The ability to convey ideas, listen actively, and adapt one's communication style to different audiences can significantly impact personal and professional success. Additionally, strong communication skills are essential for problem solving, conflict resolution, and leadership, making them invaluable across various contexts. In a world that often prizes politeness over authenticity, the art of honest communication and conversations can seem both revolutionary and daunting. Yet it is within these candid exchanges, especially when they are difficult, unpopular, and challenging, that the true impact is forged.

This chapter explores the transformative power of straightforward communication—the courage it requires and the profound changes it can bring.

We'll discuss being honest, even when it's painful, and finding the bravery to express your truth. Throughout my life, I've studied communication by watching videos of entrepreneurs, reading books, and listening to audiobooks. Improving my own communication style, tone, and manner is an ongoing personal passion.

Undertaking this research has helped me understand that being clear, concise, and direct is crucial. Mastering communication can create positive change in our own lives, as well as the lives of others.

KEEPING THINGS SIMPLE: THE POWER OF CLEAR COMMUNICATIONS

The best communicators use simple language, aided by tips and techniques that help them convey the right message so that delivery is actually understood and people listen. Your words really do matter. Especially in a rapidly changing world where opinions matter, having a foundation of good communication to nurture relationships and build positive bonds is a wonderful skill, and something that's needed by all of us.

It's incredibly important to be vulnerable and honest. Take a step back and think about a time when you've had to deliver a tough message, or entered a difficult conversation:

- How did you communicate?
- How did you feel ahead of the conversation?
- How did you feel during and after the conversation?
- Did you land the message as clearly as you could have?
- Did the recipient walk away with a clear understanding of your message?

And, more importantly:

- Did you actually get to the point?

On the flip side, consider a time when you communicated brilliantly, where people understood the topic, your intent, and your point, walking away with absolute clarity. How did you feel during that conversation? And how did you feel afterwards?

How often do you *really* think about what you have to say, or what you're about to say? We've probably all been in a position where we've said something on the spur of the moment. We've dropped an email very quickly because we're too busy to think, or delivered a communication during a meeting before realising afterwards that it was incorrect or poorly phrased. If that's happened to you, you probably put your head in your hands and thought: 'Oh my God, there could have been a much better way of doing that.'

I remember being called into a meeting at the 11th hour to provide some perspective on a project we were about to start. This was exciting because many senior leaders were in the room, but I felt completely unprepared. (You may be able to relate.) There I was, young, brash, confident, ready to go, and taking on the challenge of this meeting. I thought I had it nailed—but when I entered the meeting, nerves kicked in. Everyone looked at me as I sat down, before eventually delivering the required facts and information. I could feel myself waffling and see people rolling their eyes, crossing their arms, and just looking at me as if to say: 'What are you going on about? Get to the point.' While I was learning fast at that time, I had an unfortunate tendency of going through all the details. When I came out of the meeting, I realised they didn't want every single detail; instead, they just wanted a *precis* of the project status—and I failed.

I then went into a meeting room with a couple of colleagues, put my head in my hands, and started talking about how I felt about the situation and how I thought I was going to get fired. They started giving me a lot of advice, saying 'Maybe you could have done this,' 'Maybe you could have prepared better,' 'Maybe you could have just not said this or not said that,' etc. They offered so much guidance that although I was already frustrated coming out of the meeting, they made it worse. But it wasn't really their fault. I didn't actually say I just wanted to sit there and rant, and for them to listen. They thought I wanted their advice, and obviously got frustrated because I wasn't listening. It was a whole spiral of bad communication and poor messaging that day, which I'll never forget. Since then, I've started to think hard about how to communicate the message, what to say, and how to deliver it. Even if it *is* an 11th-hour ask, I'd process that in my mind very quickly and make sure I get to the point—by including a clear title, intention, and expectation.

THE IMPORTANCE OF BUILDING TRUST AND CONNECTION THROUGH HONEST COMMUNICATION

Honest communication is the foundation of any strong relationship, whether personal or professional. By expressing thoughts and feelings transparently, we foster an environment of trust and openness. But honesty is not just about speaking the truth; it also involves being vulnerable, expressing our thoughts and feelings authentically, and embracing the discomfort that often accompanies difficult conversations.

Imagine a workplace where team members feel free to voice their concerns about a project without fear of retribution. Picture friendships where both parties can discuss their disagreements openly, leading to mutual understanding and growth. Whenever individuals feel safe to share their true selves, it leads to more meaningful connections.

These scenarios are not just idealistic; they are achievable when we commit to being honest, even when it's hard.

I recall working on a big partnership programme, aiming to contract a new partner for our loyalty scheme. Months of hard work had gone into this project, and we were 80% there—not 100%—with the detail. At that time, the leaders were always striving for perfection. My project team were fearful of sharing their concerns, but I felt it was time to talk with the senior stakeholders to share where we were on the project, where the gaps were, and what we had to do going forward. I explained quite clearly that we had to change key processes, and needed more budget to deliver on some of the commitments that had been made due to increasing supplier costs. I also shared concerns about some of the other functions that were behind schedule, and those where I sensed a lack of ownership and accountability.

There was stunned silence for a minute. People stared at me.

I thought, it's all over. They're going to close down the project, or replace me as Project Director. The Board understood, actually applauding my straightforwardness. Because I demonstrated what was missing, they now understand where the gaps are and what they had to do to support the project and make it successful.

FINDING THE STRENGTH TO SPEAK UP

I had the courage to be straightforward. While it takes courage to be able to speak our truth and vulnerability, most people tend to shy away from that. If you actually practise this on a regular basis, it can really help you change for the better. Being straightforward is a form of bravery, challenging us to confront our fears of rejection, conflict, and change.

Often we shy away from honest conversations because we anticipate negative reactions. However, it is essential to remember that while we cannot control how others respond, we can control our approach and intentions.

Consider the following strategies to cultivate courage in your own conversations:

- **Embrace vulnerability, acknowledging your own uncertainties and fears.** By sharing these feelings, you

create a safe space for others to do the same, fostering an environment where honest dialogue can flourish.
- **Practise active listening when engaging in difficult conversations.** Focus on truly understanding the other person's perspective. This not only demonstrates respect, but also encourages openness in return.
- **Prepare for the uncomfortable.** Anticipate the potential reactions to your honesty. Mentally rehearse the conversation, considering how you might respond to defensiveness or disagreement. This preparation can help reduce your anxiety while increasing your confidence.
- **Be clear and direct.** Use simple, straightforward language, avoiding euphemisms or vague statements that may dilute your message. Clarity is key to ensuring your intentions are understood.

One of the most challenging things to do is navigating difficult conversations. These are often the most impactful, as they challenge our assumptions, encourage growth, and drive change. Here are some common scenarios where honest communication can create significant shifts.

- Addressing conflicts directly can prevent resentment from festering by openly discussing different viewpoints. You can often find common ground and solutions that work for everyone by providing constructive feedback in both personal and professional settings.
- Offering feedback, which is essential for growth. Approach these conversations with empathy, ensuring that your intent is to support improvement rather than criticise.

- Expressing your needs and boundaries, whether in relationships or work environments, is important in articulating your needs and setting boundaries.

In our current world, where you're rushing from 30-minute meetings to hours-long meetings back to back, you have very little time to pause and reflect before each conversation.

It is critical, then, to make sure you have a little bit of reflection time before you enter back-to-back meetings. Because your brain doesn't work fast enough to keep processing all that diverse information, very often you're not thinking straight as you enter the virtual or physical room. In the first 10–15 minutes going from one meeting to another, your brain craves nourishment. It's exhausted taking on all that information, so you are just thinking about what to say instead of listening to your audience.

Effective communication involves active, attentive listening and speaking at the right moment. As someone who loves to talk, I've had to learn to control what I say, as well as how and when—moving from a rushed, direct manner to a calmer, more collected approach.

Over the last 10 years, I've invested heavily in my own self-development, especially in refining my communication skills as a coach and mentor. Mastering the art of listening intently and delivering messages with intentionality has been a key focus.

THE SINGLE BIGGEST PROBLEM IS THE ILLUSION THAT COMMUNICATION HAS TAKEN PLACE

Often we walk away after communication has taken place, thinking we've done our job. But most of the audience are left scratching their heads, wondering what actually happened there, without having grasped what we wanted to say. I'm partial to a quote by George Bernard Shaw, which says: 'The single biggest problem in communication is the illusion that it has taken place.'

The objective of the below exercise is to prepare for and effectively manage challenging conversations with confidence and clarity.

- **Define the conversation.** Write down the specific topic you need to discuss. (I emphasise 'topic' because it's important for people to know what the topic is.) Be clear about what makes this conversation difficult for you.
- **Identify your goal.** Determine what you hope to achieve from this conversation. Write down your main objectives—for example, to express your feelings, reach a resolution, understand the other person's perspective, and so forth.
- **Prepare your points.** List the key points you want to communicate. Focus on the facts, your feelings, and how the situation affects you, along with any solutions or compromises you'd like to propose.

- **Anticipate reactions.** Think about how the other person might respond. Write down possible reactions and how you might address them. Consider what questions might they ask, and what objections might they raise. How would you stay calm and focused if the conversation becomes emotional?
- **Practise, practise, practise active listening.** Remind yourself of the importance of listening. Write down a few active listening techniques you can use during the conversation, such as nodding to show understanding, or paraphrasing what the other person says to confirm understanding. Also consider asking open-ended questions to encourage dialogue.
- **Role-play (optional).** If possible, practice the conversation with a friend or family member. Role-playing can help you feel more comfortable and confident.
- **Set a positive intention before the conversation.** Write down a statement that reflects your desire for the constructive outcome, e.g.: 'I aim to communicate openly and respectfully. I want to understand the other person's perspective while sharing my own.'

This exercise can help you navigate difficult conversations with greater ease and effectiveness over time. I recommend watching the 2020 TEDx talk by Keisha Brewer called 'It's Not Manipulation, It's Strategic Communication.'

Keisha challenges the common notion that 'It's not what you say, it's how you say it.' She argues that what you say is just as important as how you deliver it—this is the essence of strategic communication.

We've all been in situations where we've tried to explain something to family, colleagues, or a boss, only for them to not understand. We get frustrated, wondering why they're not 'getting it'.

Keisha's insights shed light on this issue. Effective communication requires thoughtfulness about both content and delivery. By mastering strategic communication, you can navigate tricky conversations with more clarity and impact.

And quite often, the communication style doesn't follow what you need to become a strategic communicator. Strategic communication allows you to get what you want out of life, so it's really important. There's a technique behind it. But what *is* strategic communication? We've probably all read various books with highly technical language explaining what it is, but that's not it; what Keisha actually refers to is simply communicating.

Conversely, strategic communication is communicating with purpose while showcasing value in order to achieve a goal. Strategic communication actually means that both parties feel they're getting something good out of the deal.

So, how do you deliver strategic communication effectively?

- Identify the goal.

- Understand your audience.
- Communicate the value.
- Express the need.

This method will help you combat resistance when you're communicating challenges or having difficult conversations.

When I was Marketing Director, we were negotiating (or my team was negotiating) a major insurance deal for a credit card product portfolio. My team had gone through rounds of conversations, and the right outcome just wasn't being delivered for both parties.

Eventually, I got involved. We sat down with files of paperwork, and slide after slide of PowerPoint. To me, it all got very confusing. There was a lot of communication, extensive meeting notes, and people talking around the table over each other. It all just seemed messy and confusing. The noise meant that nobody was really paying attention to what was actually needed as the goal.

I encouraged the team to take a step back and identify the goal. What were we trying to achieve? We wanted to secure a reduced cost for the global insurance policy while remaining in a strong relationship with the same service provider. We then needed to understand their needs through asking the right questions about what they wanted from the deal.

When we then began discussing the value, we soon realised that 'value' to them involved the term of the contract. They were willing to reduce the price (which was the value to us) for a longer term. We then expressed our importance to each other as strategic partners; we found common ground, creating a win–win situation overall. This happened by simplifying communication and making sure everybody understood exactly what our goal was, what the audience needed, what the value was, and what the outcome should be.

After six to nine months of negotiation, we got there in the end.

THE CHALLENGE OF BREAKING DOWN BARRIERS WITH OPEN COMMUNICATION AT HOME

I went to school and college while everyone else was at work, came home, and talked about normal things. Nobody really discussed what was going on deep inside, what their problems were, or the challenges they had faced. I remember one day, after achieving incredibly bad results in my O-Level exams, I had a choice to make: Either retake the exams or get a job. I wanted to pursue the latter, so before I retook the exams I had a conversation with my grandfather, explaining where I felt I went wrong. My intent was to agree with his mindset that I shouldn't carry on, because if I went to work, I could start earning some money (just like my father did). If you recall, my focus and ambition at that time was to earn more cash so I could start taking care of the family. Yet I knew this was going to be a difficult conversation, because my grandfather's ambition was to get me through higher education, which meant getting to university and finishing my degree.

I started my conversation with him by saying: 'What's the point? I'm not good at this, but I can go and work and earn money instead.' I tried to sell him on the idea that I could contribute to the household expenses, similar to how my father worked with him many years ago, where he was also making an important contribution to the family expenses and bills. Maybe I was trying to step into my father's footsteps too early. Anyway, I explained my side of things. I don't believe I set the right goal or demonstrated value, so the conversation did not go well. He looked at me and said, 'I don't understand.' So, I tried to explain again that I didn't want to carry on with the exams and further education. I could feel myself unravelling by this point, thinking this conversation wasn't going anywhere.

He looked at me and said, 'That's not an option. You will carry on, and you're not giving up. You are going to do your exams again, and you're going to get through this time by working hard.'

He reminded me that life was difficult and it was getting harder, so having a good education behind me will get me through the rest of my life. He wasn't wrong. I bought into this idea at that moment. He sold me the value of carrying on with my education, and he created that need.

Navigating difficult conversations has been a lifelong journey for me. I haven't always been honest, often staying quiet to avoid causing more problems. What I really needed was to be brave and authentic.

I strive to embody that bravery and authenticity today. Modelling this inspires others to do the same. This ripple effect can lead to a culture of openness, where individuals feel empowered to share. In such an environment, innovation thrives, collaboration flourishes, and community strengthens.

Engaging in honest communication also equips us with the tools to navigate the constant changes we face in daily life. By embracing vulnerability and directness, we can tackle challenges head-on.

When you are communicating with anyone, use the **60 second tip rule**. Think about the **topic**, making sure it's clear and the audience knows exactly what you want to talk about. Then think about the **intent**. What is your intention? What do you need the audience to do? Is it for them to make a decision? To listen? To take it away and reflect? Then, think about the **point**. What is the point you're trying to make? Get to it as quickly as you can, because that's where you take action—and that's where you'll feel progress being made.

The reference to the 60-second tip can be found in Chris Fenning's 2025 TEDx talk, *The 60 Seconds that Make or Break a Conversation*.

CONCLUSION

As we embrace the journey of having conversations and making sure we can communicate with impact, the journey of honest communication is not a destination, but an ongoing process that never stops. It requires constant practice, self-reflection, and a willingness to face discomfort. However, the rewards are immeasurable. By embracing honesty, we create a life rich with meaningful connections, foster an environment of trust, and empower ourselves and others to adapt to the changes life brings.

As you reflect on your communication style, consider the conversations you could have, what you may have been avoiding, what truths are waiting to be expressed, and what impact your honesty could have had. On those around you, remember the most profound change often begins with a single brave conversation. Take that step, then watch as the world around you transforms.

My 'tough love' messages for you:

- Your intentions matter, but they mean nothing without clarity—so don't ever assume anything, but tell people directly instead.
- Avoiding difficult conversations only breeds resentment, so always have the courage to communicate even when it's uncomfortable.
- Your feelings are valid, but they don't matter if you can't express them clearly. So don't hold back—be direct.

It's important to communicate clearly to your audience that the communication journey is an ongoing process, which is set to become even more complicated with AI. This innovation is making our world a faster, smarter place, but it's also putting more pressure on us to communicate faster, more meaningfully, through different channels, and in a new language we all need to understand.

AI is changing the world we live in, so let's see how we should embrace it.

CHAPTER 12

THE DOUBLE-EDGED SWORD OF AI: HOPE, EXCITEMENT AND FEAR

'EMBRACE THE TECHNOLOGIES OF TODAY, AS THEY HOLD THE KEYS FOR TOMORROW.'

AI has infiltrated our world, becoming deeply integrated into our daily lives. From limited understanding to ubiquitous presence, AI now streamlines our routines, provides us with instant information, and transforms how we communicate and do business.

Yet, this rapid advancement has sparked a spectrum of emotions—excitement, hope, anxiety, and fear. This chapter explores AI's profound impact on our lives, particularly its complex relationship with mental health, as individuals confront the fear of job loss, societal change, and diminishing human connections. The 'fear of becoming obsolete' (FOBO) has emerged as a prominent concern.

We will cover how AI is changing the world we live in, and the fact you have to embrace it.

EMBRACING THE FUTURE: THE RISE OF AI IN OUR DAILY LIVES

As AI emerged, its presence evolved from subtle to pervasive. From virtual assistants to algorithm-curated feeds, AI began shaping experiences in unnoticed ways. Daily tasks became streamlined and chores automated, freeing people to pursue their own enjoyment.

Soon, AI systems handled the mundane, reducing human interaction in areas like customer service and manufacturing. Many companies now leverage AI to service customers, making direct human interaction increasingly rare.

The rapid advancement of AI is leaving many feeling vulnerable about their future and job security. I reflect on conversations with my grandfather, who took pride in his 45-year career at Barclays. 'A job at a bank,' he'd say, 'is secure for life.' How times have changed, as AI displaces many from banking roles.

The era of the 'job for life' my grandfather so firmly believed in is now over. The speed of AI's evolution has disrupted long-held assumptions about career stability. This shift has sown widespread uncertainty about the future of work.

Nowadays, people develop squiggly careers, jumping from one business to another to improve their remuneration, their competencies, and their capabilities to grow personally and professionally. Staying with the same organisation now very rarely helps you reap larger rewards and annual increments when compared to moving around every three or four years. Let me ask you: How many people do you know who have been in their jobs for 20, 30, 40 years? Probably not many. People don't just move jobs because of AI; humans are now more exposed to new opportunities (AI has made this happen) and patience is now a rare commodity. After all, we all want everything to be faster and more convenient.

This book is all about building resilience through action, enabling you to achieve your ambitions. AI can absolutely support this journey, and if you are not learning about AI and how it can enhance your life, my recommendation is to stop making excuses and get on with it. If you don't learn and build your capabilities, AI will directly affect your mental health—the anxiety associated with potential unemployment leads to stress, depression, and a sense of hopelessness. In recent times, I have encountered many individuals who dedicated years to mastering their crafts, only to suddenly find themselves displaced and questioning their value in a rapidly changing landscape. This is particularly pronounced in sectors heavily reliant on routine tasks.

ADAPTING AND THRIVING IN A WORLD OF TRANSFORMATION

Change is inevitable, impacting the familiar routines of life. During the pandemic in 2020 we had a new normal way of being, and now we have a new normal dictated by technology. This constant state of flux contributes to our collective sense of instability and uncertainty. Many people are suffering from 'techno stress', with individuals feeling compelled to continuously learn and adapt to new tools and platforms. While beneficial in the long run, this often results in burnout. It's the relentless pursuit of staying relevant in a digital age which is taking a toll on mental wellbeing, as many experience feelings of inadequacy when comparing themselves to their tech-savvy peers. This leads to diminishing human connections.

THE VITAL ROLE OF HUMAN CONNECTIONS IN AN AI-DRIVEN ERA

My entire world is now focused on building and creating better human connections. Human connection is vital in today's world to improve our own mental wellbeing and the way we live our lives.

Alongside the anxieties of job loss and change, the rise of AI is influencing the nature of human connections. As technology increasingly facilitates communication through screens rather than in-person interactions, many individuals report feelings of isolation. Mental health and wellbeing struggles have surged as individuals grapple with the emotional toll of constantly seeking validation online, or have no desire to commute on crowded transportation services, or have lost the ability to communicate in person. The prediction is that up to 75% of the workforce will experience some kind of mental health and wellbeing issue by the end of 2026.

This is a massive challenge for business leaders today: How to build high-performance, high-impact teams and seek out new perspectives when people don't want to socialise together at work. Many companies have tried to force the issue, asking employees to attend the office in person for x days per week, while leaders have experienced a backlash from their employees who now seek a better work/life balance. Many of the younger generations prioritise work/life balance over salary and are prepared to switch jobs to get it.

It is not easy being a business leader right now, and managing change has given rise to more 'change fatigue'—especially as the pressure is building from all sides (your employees, your executive board, your investors, and your customers). With little time to think through the challenges, many of us lean on AI to help out…but AI takes away your ability to think. I often think back to my conversations with my grandfather, who used to tell me how he wrote ledgers for Barclays and did all his sums in his head. Imagine what he would say now. He would push me to add up in my head when I was at school, which put me under real pressure—kids of today have it so much easier in terms of access to tools, but how are they pushing their own learning boundaries without the help of automated systems?

FINDING HARMONY, BALANCING AI INTEGRATION WITH MEANINGFUL HUMAN INTERACTION

Challenges persist as AI further infiltrates our lives. Accept not knowing everything, and strive for balanced coexistence. Understanding mental health's importance amid technological change is crucial.

Awareness campaigns and education can empower individuals to thrive alongside AI, not be overshadowed. Online platforms for mental health support and peer interaction can mitigate isolation, but face-to-face connections remain vital for nurturing genuine relationships.

It's far from easy as we navigate the complexities of AI's impact on daily life and mental health—clearly, technology serves as both a tool and a challenge. The fears surrounding job losses, accelerating change, and diminished human connections are valid and must be addressed with empathy and understanding by fostering resilience and encouraging meaningful connections. Society can harness the benefits of AI while safeguarding mental wellbeing.

NAVIGATING THE AI LANDSCAPE WITHOUT BEING AN EXPERT

I understand AI and what it can do, but I'm not an expert on all the different AI apps, tools, and solutions. There are experts out there who can help you, however, so be aware of what works for you and then learn and explore with AI—it's all about trial and error. You'll get some things right and some things wrong; sometimes it will work for you, while other times it won't.

If you want to learn new skills, you can also start a different career. AI can help you navigate to new sectors and new capabilities, even after 15 or 20 years of time investment with one organisation. It's never too late to learn or start something new. All it takes is your passion, drive and commitment, your self-belief, and your willingness to take action.

Let's do a small exercise now.

What 3 concerns do you have about AI?	What can you do to overcome these concerns?	Who can support you?

We know AI can negatively impact the human brain and emotional wellbeing in several ways, primarily through its influence on attention, social interactions, and mental health. Let me cover these three areas in a little bit more detail:

- **Reduced attention span.** The constant influx of information and stimuli from AI-driven tech like social media can reduce attention spans. This encourages skimming over deep reading and critical thinking. As we grow accustomed to rapid content consumption, our ability to focus and engage in sustained mental effort diminishes. This can lead to frustration when tackling complex tasks—a concerning loss of our ability to think problems through in detail.

- **Altered social interactions.** AI often mediates social interactions through platforms that prioritise engagement over genuine connection. While these tools can keep people connected, they can also lead to superficial relationships and a lack of meaningful engagement. This reliance on digital communication fosters feelings of loneliness and isolation as individuals may struggle to form authentic connections. The curated nature of online lives can also lead to unhealthy comparisons, increasing anxiety and depression as people measure their worth against others.
- **Increased anxiety and uncertainty.** The rapid pace of AI advancement can generate anxiety about job security and the future. As individuals witness automation encroaching on various professions, concerns about obsolescence and the need to continuously adapt can be overwhelming. Remember FOBO—the fear of becoming obsolete—can contribute to stress and feelings of helplessness, impacting overall mental health. Furthermore, the pressure to keep up with technological advancements and stay relevant can lead to burnout, as individuals feel compelled to constantly learn, adapt, and keep up.

In summary:

- While AI offers numerous benefits, its negative impacts on the human brain and emotional wellbeing stem from its effects on attention, social interactions, and the anxiety it generates about the future.

- Balancing technology use with mindful practices and fostering genuine human connections can help mitigate these adverse effects. It's now the time to reduce the untold hours everyone spends on social media—after all, at the end of the day, what do you actually achieve after spending two to three hours scrolling?

Human connection is the one thing that AI cannot replace. It's incapable of replacing human relationships when you're dealing with partners and clients. When that trusted relationship is formed, it is not something that AI can overcome and replace.

Remember, talking to each other is a good thing. It's beneficial to sit around a table and engage in an actual conversation during a family dinner. It's good to pick up the phone and call someone, an activity which seems to be quite alien to many people in today's world. Connecting with other humans creates a purpose, strengthening communities while actually advancing our prosperity. Strong human connections build trusted relationships.

LEARNING FROM TECHNOLOGICAL ADVANCEMENT TO SHAPE OUR FUTURE

Reminiscing on my childhood, I'm struck by how little we discussed technological advancements back then. I wonder what GR and RG would have thought about new tech having displaced so many jobs. They likely couldn't have imagined the internet, relying instead on encyclopaedias for knowledge.

I remember our home set of encyclopaedias, sold door-to-door. That's how we gathered insights for projects. Nowadays, we have a wealth of information at our fingertips.

One conversation with my grandfather stands out. This was when I first purchased the ZX Spectrum Console and the Commodore 64 PC. I'd worked hard at a local retail business, saving my money to purchase the new tech. I remember the day I brought the systems home; I was super-proud. My grandfather felt these were just gaming machines which wouldn't really take off in the workplace or at home to manage our day-to-day lives. He saw me many times just playing games on the machines and would often remind me that he wrote out ledgers using his memory and safeguarded beautiful handwritten books, keeping those records in a library or an archive for many years as they gathered dust. The one thing I've noticed is that many people have forgotten how to write properly these days because they've become so used to just typing all of the time, either on their phone or a laptop or some other device. AI even writes your letters and communication for you, so you really don't have to think too hard.

When I graduated, I always looked for the simplest explanations, but often didn't find them. I'm not sure why we have all become obsessed with complexity, as it has made our world a difficult place to navigate. I have now come out of the corporate world after 30 blissful years, and AI has played a massive role in my career advancement in the last five or six. I've become a data geek—not in the sense of an analyst, but I loved what data could actually show, the trends, the insights and fast results. I was working in an environment where I was helping influence shopper behaviour, encouraging shoppers to buy additional products, revisit stores, or make additional purchases online with personalised offers. Understanding shopper behaviour by utilising AI tools gave me a real buzz.

As an entrepreneur, I've started using AI tools to help organise my business. The one area I loathe is admin, so I now use AI tools to manage the admin tasks, enabling me to focus on the important matters like business growth and client relationships. I have no appetite to grow a huge organization with thousands of people, but I *do* want to create a successful global business, and use as many relevant AI tools as possible, and have the right talented people in place who understand how to use these tools and solutions to scale the business. Well, that's the ambition.

EMPOWERING OURSELVES: TAKING CHARGE OF OUR RELATIONSHIP WITH AI

Embracing AI and feeling more in control of the changes it brings can be achieved through a few important actions.

- **Continuous learning and skill development.** One of the most empowering ways to embrace AI is by committing to lifelong learning, which involves actively seeking out educational resources, such as online courses, workshops and certifications, that focus on AI technologies and their applications. Staying informed about industry trends can also help you understand how AI may impact specific sectors, allowing for informed decision-making and career planning.

- **Leveraging AI as a tool for enhancement.** Rather than viewing AI as a threat, it's beneficial to see it as a tool that can augment human capabilities. Embracing AI technologies in daily tasks can lead to increased efficiency and productivity. You can harness its potential to improve outcomes while allowing more time for creative and strategic pursuits.
- **Building a supportive community.** Engaging with a network of like-minded individuals can foster a sense of control and support in navigating the changes brought by AI. Joining professional groups, attending industry events, or participating in online forums can facilitate the exchange of ideas and experiences. These connections can provide insights into best practices, opportunities for collaboration, and a collective understanding of how to adapt to AI advancements.

By focusing on continuous learning, leveraging AI as an enhancement tool, and building a supportive community, you can embrace AI with confidence and a sense of empowerment at the end of the day. Saying 'I can't' or 'I won't' is a self-imposed barrier—so break it down, giving yourself the chance to thrive in the modern era.

LET ME GIVE YOU SOME AI 'TOUGH LOVE' MESSAGES

- Complacency is the enemy of progress. If you're not evolving, you're regressing—so challenge yourself to learn and adapt, starting today.
- Get off social media, where you are probably consuming many wasted hours—do something useful instead.
- Spend one hour per day on a new skill or topic, then become an expert in five years or less. (Five years means 1,250 hours of expert time invested.) Sticking to what you know now will mean getting left behind.

The world is changing, so adapt or be left in the dust. AI is rapidly moving on from generative AI to *agentic* AI, which acts like an employee and delivers tangible outcomes at a fraction of the cost. Imagine, AI that thinks and acts like an employee is here already—that's a scary thought, right?

So if you are in senior/middle management, especially retail, brand, marketing, planning, supply, finance, HR, sales, or analytics (I am sure I have missed a few), AI is coming after your job. If your organisation is looking to become more profitable, they will be looking at their options to get things done faster and cheaper (often at one-hundredth the cost of an employee). Imagine the benefit for senior leaders, who have fewer employee-related challenges coupled with an always-on workforce.

If you're not working in an environment which provides instant results, then you're going to get left behind. The future is an age of instant results—in other words, Software As A Service is transitioning to **Results As A Service (RAAS)**. This is Agentic AI at its best and has been referenced in detail in Mindvalley's 2025 YouTube video *Results As A Service – The Future of AI*, and you'll be inspired what tomorrow will bring to the world.

CALMING YOUR MIND WITH PRACTICAL EXERCISES TO MANAGE YOUR AI-RELATED ANXIETY

Let me share a couple of exercises that might be able to help you navigate your world with AI.

MINDFUL REFLECTION: 10–15 MINUTES

- Find a quiet, comfortable space where you won't be disturbed, and sit down.
- Take a few deep breaths to centre yourself, acknowledging your feelings.
- Write down any specific thoughts or feelings you have about AI, including what worries you and what excites you. Allow yourself to express these feelings without judgement, then shift your perspective.
- Take a moment to reflect on the positive aspects of AI. Write down three ways AI can improve daily life or contribute positively to you and society. Consider the ways in which technology has historically evolved and how society has adapted.

- Take a few deep breaths. Inhale deeply for four seconds, hold for another four, and exhale for six. Repeat this three times, engaging your senses as you do it.
- List three things you can see, hear, and feel in your current environment. This helps bring you back to the present moment.
- Set your intentions by writing down what you would like to learn about AI. For example, set an intention to approach your feelings with curiosity instead of fear.
- Consider small, manageable steps you can take to educate yourself about AI. This could include reading articles, watching documentaries, or discussing it with knowledgeable friends.
- Finally, close with positivity. Finish the exercise by writing down one thing you're grateful for in your life right now, reflecting on how you can channel that gratitude into a positive perspective.

This exercise will help you cultivate a healthier relationship with AI, transforming anxiety into a sense of curiosity and understanding.

ROUTINE TASK EXERCISE

- Identify day-to-day tasks that you typically find boring or uninspiring.
- Then look on the internet, asking questions about which AI tool can help you simplify those tools and get those

tasks done more efficiently. You'll be surprised what you can learn really fast, and how quickly you get used to using these tools daily.

I leave you with a few final thoughts.

- Sticking to what you know will absolutely leave you behind in the long run..
- Stay ahead of the game. Invest time learning and adapting.
- The world will continue to change at a faster rate than you can keep up, so you need to adapt or you're going to get left in the dust. Ignoring AI tech advances is your own choice, no one else's.

The only person who will make your skills become obsolete is yourself, so adapt or be dragged kicking and screaming into a new world. Again, that's your choice—but the consequences are absolutely real.

Fear comes from inexperience. You may be afraid because you haven't done it yet, not because you can't do it. There are five things you need to quit right now:

1. Stop pleasing everyone.
2. Don't be afraid of change.
3. Stop living in the past and thinking too far forward.
4. Quit negative self-talk.
5. Stop overthinking things.

Have the courage to act and Unplug YANGA (Your Actions Nourish Growth Ambitions) to unveil your new world today. The road ahead might be lonely, but it will be worth it.

CONCLUSION

YANGA Unplugged shows you how to take control of your life by focusing on actions, building self-belief and resilience, and creating surroundings which boost positive energy. When you *don't* act, you are actually saying 'Yes' to comfort, 'Yes' to delay, and 'Yes' to the version of you that doesn't move quickly and decisively. Your inaction is still a decision, and it compounds—84% of long-term regrets are about things people didn't do. Clarity doesn't come from thinking; it comes from *doing*. If you wait until you are ready, you will wait for the rest of your life. The world rewards those who act, so take action today.

Put yourself first and make choices which lead you towards unlocking your dreams and achieving your ambitions—the truth is, no one else will do this for you. If you overthink what others might say, you will stand still. Everyone has an opinion, and many people will judge what you do and how you do it (that's human nature)…but it's *your* life to live, so live every day like it's your last day on earth.

I hope my stories and techniques resonate with you, inspiring you to create new momentum. Remember, the only person who creates limiting beliefs is you, and the only person who can take action to reduce or even remove limiting beliefs is you. So, find your courage, accept the outcomes, and live your best life.

My purpose is to inspire and improve the quality of life of as many people as I can. If you want to further your conversation, take your first step by reaching out—then, let's build a new connection.

YANGA: Your Actions Nourish Growth Ambitions.

WORKS CITED

Andrillon, Thomas et al. "Predicting Lapses of Attention with Sleep-Like Slow Waves." Nature Communications, June 29, 12, https://doi.org/10.1038/s41467-021-23890-7

Brewer, Keisha. "It's Not Manipulation, It's Strategic Communication." *YouTube,* uploaded by TEDx Talks, 10 January 2020, https://www.youtube.com/watch?v=QGeHS4jO0X0.

Cooper, Rebecca et al. "Associations of Changes in Sleep and Emotional and Behavioural Problems From Late Childhood to Early Adolescence." *JAMA Psychiatry,* June 1, *80*(6), 585–96.

Fenning, Chris. "The 60 Seconds that Make or Break a Conversation." *YouTube*, uploaded by TedX Talks, 19 March 2025, https://www.youtube.com/watch?v=rpFmRq5KeJs

Galloway, Scott. "How Successful People Deal With Setbacks." *YouTube*, uploaded by CNBC Make It, 9 March 2019, https://www.youtube.com/watch?v=tA7iCb9_YXc.

Leger, Kate, Charles, Susan, Turiano, Nicholas, and Almeida, David. (2016). "Personality and Stressor-Related Affect." *Journal of Personality and Social Psychology*, Jan 21, *111*(6), 917–928.

Mindvalley. "Results as a Service – The Future of AI." *YouTube*, uploaded by eStreetSecurity, 29 January 2025, https://www.youtube.com/watch?v=kAcXrfZ9dtE

Riet, Connie. "Find Mental Clarity and Declutter Your Mind: Mental Minimalism." *YouTube*, uploaded by Connie Reit, 29 April 2022, https://www.youtube.com/watch?v=PD8ZOStq6_g.

Seelye, Adriana et al. (2015). "The Impact of Sleep on Neuropsychological Performance in Cognitively Intact Older Adults." *Clinical Neuropsychology*, *29*(1), 53–66.

Shoenthal, Amy. "Navigating Setbacks: Turning Obstacles to Opportunities." *YouTube*, uploaded by TEDx Talks, 29 Jan 2025, https://www.youtube.com/watch?v=CrEhGIBCAPU.

AUTHOR BIO

Premal Patel is a dynamic new author who masterfully blends storytelling with business impact, drawing on his extensive 30-year corporate career. Having overcome life's challenges, he offers a unique perspective on business literature. Known for his action-focused mindset, Prem excels at nurturing high-performance teams and inspiring others to achieve remarkable results. His compelling narratives entertain and empower professionals to embrace challenges, helping them thrive in life.

Through his writing, Prem aims to share lessons learned and ignite a passion for excellence in others.

Connect with him by:

Email
info@yangaunplugged.com

Website links
www.tkopworld.com

www.premalpatel.co.uk
www.tkopworld.healthymindsclub.com
www.theartbrewery.com
www.ailignifi.co

LinkedIn
www.linkedin.com/in/premalpatel1

Instagram
@premalrpatel – https://www.instagram.com/premalrpatel/
@yangaunplugged – https://www.instagram.com/yangaunplugged/

RESOURCES AND IMPORTANT LINKS

At TKOP World Ltd, we are passionate about unlocking your potential and your team's performance by focusing on creating and building better human connections through business, leadership, and career coaching and applying unique practical programmes which drive performance and achieve transformational results.

www.tkopworld.com

In today's world, doing what you've always done gets you what you've always got. Our unique platform blends diverse expertise and experience of creating and growing talented individuals and high-performance teams with the science of positive psychology, wellbeing, and wellness by providing personalised solutions to every Club Member—you choose what's right for you! We provide experts and resources based on your individual or company values and needs. You gain access to a broad range of practitioners focussed on preventing stress to promote success, along with courses, workshops, videos, health testing, spa days, and retreats and discounts off hundreds of brands.

www.tkopworld.healthymindsclub.com

We support organisations, rebuild human connections, nurture trust, and create workplaces where every voice matters. Human connection is the foundation of thriving teams. We build stronger teams and smarter leaders through structured workshops focused on 'Leading with Trust', 'Seeking New Perspectives', and 'Creating Workplace Vitality'—all delivered by our unique 'Mysteries in Colour' methodology.

www.theartbrewery.com

Transform your culture and elevate your results. Alignifi is the only solution that turns organisational alignment into competitive advantage. We provide the insights and actions needed to transform your culture and results with real-time performance measurement.

www.alignifi.co

www.ingramcontent.com/pod-product-compliance
Lightning Source LLC
Chambersburg PA
CBHW020527080526
44583CB00013B/774